A New Star-Rating System
& Other Exciting News
from Frommer's!

In our continuing effort to publish the savviest, most up-to-date, and most appealing travel guides available, we've added some great new features.

Frommer's guides now include a new **star-rating system**. Every hotel, restaurant, and attraction is rated from 0 to 3 stars to help you set priorities and organize your time.

We've also added **seven brand-new features** that point you to the great deals, in-the-know advice, and unique experiences that separate travelers from tourists. Throughout the guide look for:

Finds	Special finds—those places only insiders know about
Fun Fact	Fun facts—details that make travelers more informed and their trips more fun
Kids	Best bets for kids—advice for the whole family
Moments	Special moments—those experiences that memories are made of
Overrated	Places or experiences not worth your time or money
Tips	Insider tips—some great ways to save time and money
Value	Great values—where to get the best deals

Frommer's®

PORTABLE

Whistler

1st Edition

by Constance Brissenden

WILEY
Independent Thinkers

Toronto ON

About the Author

Constance Brissenden, BA, MA, has written about British Columbia for more than 20 years. She lives in Vancouver, B.C. Additional research by Trude Huebner, Larry Loyie, James Oakes, Cora Yee.

Published by:
John Wiley & Sons Canada, Ltd.
22 Worcester Road
Etobicoke, ON M9W 1L1

National Library of Canada Cataloguing in Publication Data
Brissenden, Connie, 1947–   .
    Constance Brissenden.—1st ed.

Includes index.
ISBN 1–894413–43–1

1. Whistler Region (B.C.)—Guidebooks. I. Title.
II. Title: Portable Whistler

FC3849.W44A3 2002   917.11'31   C2002–901901–X
F1089.5.W48B75 2002

Editorial Director: Joan Whitman
Associate Editor: Melanie Rutledge
Publishing Services Director: Karen Bryan
Cartographer: Mapping Specialists, Ltd.
Illustrations: Frommer's US and Bart Vallecoccia Illustration
Text layout: IBEX Graphic Communications
Cover design: Kyle Gell
Front cover photo: J.A. Kraulis/Masterfile

Special Sales

Fer reseller information, including discounts and premium sales, please call our sales department: Tel.: 416-646-4584. For press review copies, author interviews, or other publicity information, please contact our marketing department: Tel.: 416-646-4584; Fax.: 416-646-4448.

1 2 3 4 5 TRI 06 05 04 03 02

Manufactured in Canada

Contents

List of Maps

An Invitation to the Reader

In researching this book, we discovered many wonderful places—hotels, restaurants, shops, and more. We're sure you'll find others. Please tell us about them, so we can share the information with your fellow travelers in upcoming editions. If you were disappointed with a recommendation, we'd love to know that, too. Please write to:

Frommer's Portable Whistler, 1st Edition
John Wiley & Sons Canada, Ltd. • 22 Worcester Road • Etobicoke, ON
M9W 1L1

An Additional Note

Please be advised that travel information is subject to change at any time—and this is especially true of prices. We therefore suggest that you write or call ahead for confirmation when making your travel plans. The authors, editors, and publisher cannot be held responsible for the experiences of readers while traveling. Your safety is important to us, however, so we encourage you to stay alert and be aware of your surroundings. Keep a close eye on cameras, purses, and wallets, all favorite targets of thieves and pickpockets.

What the Symbols Mean

The following abbreviations are used for credit cards:

| AE | American Express | DC | Diners Club | V | Visa |
| DISC | Discover | MC | MasterCard | | |

FROMMERS.COM

Now that you have the guidebook to a great trip, visit our website at **www.frommers.com** for travel information on nearly 2,000 destinations. With features updated regularly, we give you instant access to the most current trip-planning information available. At Frommers.com, you'll also find the best prices on air fares, accommodations, and car rentals—and you can even book travel online through our travel booking partners. At Frommers.com you'll also find the following:

- Daily Newsletter highlighting the best travel deals
- Hot Spot of the Month/Vacation Sweepstakes & Travel Photo Contest
- More than 200 Travel Message Boards
- Outspoken Newsletters and Feature Articles on travel bargains, vacation ideas, tips & resources, and more!

Here's what the critics say about Frommer's:

"Amazingly easy to use. Very portable, very complete."

—*Booklist*

"The only mainstream guide to list specific prices. The Walter Cronkite of guidebooks—with all that implies."

—*Travel & Leisure*

"Complete, concise, and filled with useful information."

—*New York Daily News*

"Hotel information is close to encyclopedic."

—*Des Moines Sunday Register*

"Detailed, accurate, and easy-to-read information for all price ranges."

—*Glamour Magazine*

Planning a Trip to Whistler

Just 35 years ago, Whistler Resort was little more than a blip on a long and bumpy road north from sea level to an elevation of 675m (2,214 ft.) in the Coast Mountains. Today, it's not only the top ski resort in North America but also a popular summer destination. The journey from Vancouver, British Columbia, your gateway city and Canada's gateway to the Pacific Rim, is now under 2 hours by car. Having visited Whistler in every season, I can also recommend the quieter months of early summer and autumn. Yes, some restaurants or attractions are closed. On the other hand, you'll find terrific deals on accommodations, and fewer people competing with you for the magnificent views on the hiking trails.

All roads lead to Whistler by way of Vancouver (unless you're coming the long way from Lillooet, BC, covered in chapter 10, "Side Trips"). The Greater Vancouver region is home to more than two million people, with all the amenities you would expect of an international center. Yet it's still only 120km (75 miles) from Whistler. Many visitors top off their trip to Whistler by spending time getting to know Vancouver as well.

1 Visitor Information

Tourism Whistler offers comprehensive travel and accommodations planning and booking online at **www.tourismwhistler.com,** or call ✆ **800/944-7853** in the US and Canada. Mailing address: Tourism Whistler, 4010 Whistler Way, Whistler, BC V0N 1B4.

The local tabloid newspaper **The Question** is online at **www.whistlerquestion.com** for information on Whistler and the nearby community of Pemberton to the north. The **Pique Newsmagazine,** a weekly entertainment and activity newspaper, is at **www.piquenewsmagazine.com.**

For free British Columbia travel information, call Supernatural British Columbia toll-free from anywhere in North America at ✆ **800/HELLOBC** (435-5622) or from Vancouver at ✆ **604/435-5622.** International visitors can call ✆ **250/387-1642.** Reservations and information are also available through www.hellobc.com; the mailing address is P.O. Box 9830 Stn. Prov. Government, Victoria, BC V8W 9W5. In England, write to Tourism BC, 3 Regent St., London, England SW1Y 4NS. From within the UK, visitors can call ✆ **0891 715000** (premium rate line).

For Vancouver information and reservations, contact **Tourism Vancouver** at ✆ **604/683-2000; www.tourismvancouver.com** (Vancouver Tourist Info Centre, 200 Burrard St., Vancouver, BC V8C 3L6).

ENTRY REQUIREMENTS   Citizens or permanent residents of the US require a birth or baptismal certificate, voter's registration card, resident alien card, green card, or passport to enter Canada. Proof of residence, such as a driver's license, should also be carried. However, this is not accepted as proof of citizenship. All other international visitors must be in possession of a valid national passport and, in some cases, a visa (check with your local Canadian Consulate or Embassy).

If you're driving from Seattle, you'll clear customs at the Peace Arch crossing (open 24 hr. a day) in Blaine, Washington. To enter Canada you will pass through **Canadian Customs** (✆ **800/461-9999** [from within Canada] and ✆ **204/983-3500** [from outside Canada]), and through **US Customs** ✆ **360/332-5771** on your departure.

If you fly directly into Vancouver International Airport from another country, you'll clear Customs in the new International Terminal. Once you get through Canada Customs passport control, you and your luggage will go through Customs before you leave the terminal. Be prepared for security delays in Customs.

When bringing children into Canada, you must have proof of legal guardianship. If you are traveling with a minor and are not the child's legal guardian, a notarized letter from the parents plus contact telephone numbers (day and evening) must be provided. If you're under 18 and not accompanied by a parent or guardian, bring a permission letter signed by your parent or legal guardian allowing you to travel to Canada. You will still need proof of sufficient funds and evidence of return transportation.

Citizens of Great Britain, Australia, and New Zealand don't require visas to enter Canada, but they must carry either a valid passport or other recognized travel document as well as evidence of funds sufficient for a temporary stay (such as credit cards).

Southwestern British Columbia

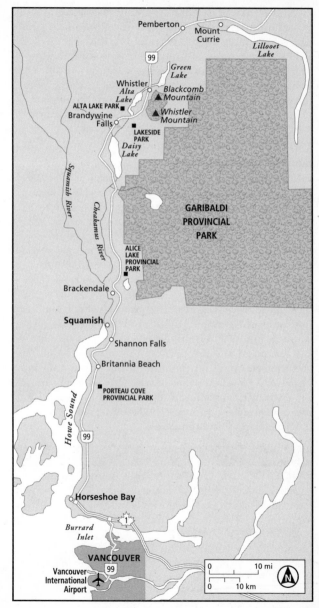

CUSTOMS REGULATIONS   If you are bringing excess luggage, be sure to carry a detailed inventory list that includes the acquisition date, serial number, and cost or replacement value of each item. It will speed things up at the border. If you are stopped, Customs will help you fill in the forms that allow you to bring in your effects temporarily, but they will require a deposit. If you are entering Canada from the US and have registered the goods with US Customs prior to entering Canada, or if an E29B form was issued, US Customs will need to see this list to check off what you take out of Canada. You will be charged Customs duties for anything left in Canada.

Some additional pointers:

- If you come from the US and bring more than US$10,000 in cash, you must file a transaction report with US Customs.
- Do not joke about carrying explosives, drugs, or other contraband. You will have your bags and person searched in detail and face arrest for conspiracy.
- Canada has strict laws concerning firearms and restricted weapons. For more information call ✆ **800/731-4000.**
- If you're bringing any prescription medicines, bring a copy of your prescription.
- Americans returning home after more than 48 hours in Canada can take US$400 worth of goods without paying duty. If you've been in Canada less than 48 hours, the maximum duty-free amount is US$200.
- For more information on coming in and going out of Canada, contact **Canada Customs—Pacific Region,** Third Floor, 333 Dunsmuir St., Vancouver, BC V6B 5R4 (✆ **800/461-9999** from within Canada and ✆ **204/983-3500** from outside Canada; **www.ccra-adrc.gc.ca**).

2 Money

CURRENCY   The Canadian currency system is decimal and resembles both British and US denominations. Canadian monetary units are dollars and cents, with bills in different colors. The standard denominations are C$5 (US$3.10), C$10 (US$6.25), C$20 (US$12.50), C$50 (US$31.25), and C$100 (US$62.50). The "loonie" (named because of the loon on one side) is the C$1 (US$.60) coin that replaced the C$1 bill. A C$2 (US$1.25) coin, called the "toonie" because it's worth two loonies, has replaced the Canadian $2 bill.

Banks and other financial institutions offer a standard rate of exchange based on the daily world monetary rate. Bank ATMs give the best exchange rates, so use them to withdraw funds. Hotels usually give a lower exchange rate. Stores and restaurants in Whistler widely accept American currency, and most will exchange amounts in excess of your dinner check or purchase. However, these establishments set their own exchange percentages, and generally offer the worst rates of all.

What Things Cost in Whistler	C$	US$
Liter of gas, Squamish	.65	.40
Liter of gas, Whistler	.70	.45
Season ski pass	1,519	949
Day skiing	61.00	38.00
Movie	10.00	6.25
Photofinishing, roll of 24, 1-hour	13.00	8.10
Gourmet juice (250ml)	3.15	1.95
Starbucks cafe latte grande	3.55	2.20
Glass of beer	5.50	3.45
Glass of wine	8.00	5.00
Evian water, 1 liter bottled	2.20	1.35
591 milliliters of Coke	1.40	.85
Three-course Dungeness crab meal	29.95	18.70
Kentucky Fried Chicken 10-piece meal	19.95	12.45
Italian sub sandwich, 8 inches	7.00	4.35
Pizza slice	3.75	2.35
Smoked salmon sandwich with cream cheese and onions	7.25	4.55
Strawberry rhubarb square	2.00	1.25
Ben & Jerry ice cream (500ml)	5.60	3.50
HABANA Julieta cigar	39	24.35
Boutique bread	4.30	2.70
White bread	1.00	.60
Whistler postcard	.60	.35
Stamp to mail to US	.65	.40
Whistler *Question* newspaper	1.00	.60
Condominium starting at	220,000	137,000
Single-family home	400,000– 8.9 million	250,000– 5.5 million
Firewood, cord	175.00	109.00

TRAVELER'S CHECKS   While ATMs are the most convenient way of obtaining local currency (and usually give the best exchange rate), some people prefer carrying traveler's checks. Traveler's checks in Canadian funds are universally accepted by banks (which may charge a small fee to cash them), larger stores, and hotels. If you carry American Express or Thomas Cook traveler's checks, you can cash them at the local offices of those companies free of charge.

ATM NETWORKS   The 24-hour PLUS and Cirrus ATM systems are available in Whistler. The systems convert Canadian withdrawals to your account's currency within 24 hours.

CREDIT & DEBIT CARDS   Major credit cards are widely accepted, especially American Express, Diners Club, MasterCard, and Visa. British debit cards such as Barclay's Visa debit card are also accepted. The amount spent in Canadian dollars will automatically be converted to your currency by your issuing company when you're billed—generally at rates that are better than what you'd receive for cash at a currency exchange.

TAXES   Most purchases in British Columbia are subject to a sales tax totaling 14% of the purchase price. The provincial sales tax (PST) of 7% applies to all retail purchases with the exception of liquor, which is taxed at 10%. The goods and services tax (GST) is a federal tax of 7% applicable to most purchased goods and services regardless of whether the buyer is a resident of Canada or a visitor to Canada.

Except for campgrounds and houseboats, tourist accommodation rates are subject to an 8% provincial hotel and motel room tax. Where approved, an additional 2% tourism tax is levied by the local municipal government.

C GST Refunds

While adding up to a lot of paperwork for very little return unless your total purchases are substantial, the Canadian government offers foreign visitors the right to claim a full rebate of GST paid on goods that they take out of the country within 60 days of purchase, and on GST paid for short-term accommodation (less than 1 month per location). Visitor rebates cannot be claimed for GST paid on alcohol, tobacco, or gasoline for personal use. Visitors departing Canada who are traveling by private vehicle or charter bus tour must have their original receipts validated by duty-free shop staff or customs officials. Visitors departing by air, rail, charter bus, or ferry must include their boarding pass or carrier ticket with their claim. Refunds are not available at the Vancouver International Airport.

In order to qualify for the GST rebate you must ensure that purchase amounts (before taxes) total at least C$200. Each individual receipt must show a minimum purchase amount (before taxes) of C$50. GST must be paid on goods.

Detailed information on the GST is available in the Revenue Canada Customs and Excise publication #177. Forms can also be obtained at major hotels and information centers and online at www.rc.gc.ca/visitors. For more information or assistance call ✆ 902/432-5608 (outside Canada) or ✆ 800/668-4748 (inside Canada), or write to Revenue Canada Customs and Excise, Visitors Rebate Program, Ottawa, ON K1A 1J5.

3 When to Go

Whistler weather is the subject of much debate. Summers are temperate but can get satisfyingly hot, ideal for swimming, biking, and mountain treks. Since you're in the mountains, nights are often cool. And, being on the "wet coast," rain does fall. Locals are quick to point out that when it's raining down below it's snowing on the mountains. Gray and even rainy days are ideal for cozying up before a fireplace or taking contemplative walks along Whistler's lake trail routes.

THE WEATHER
Daily Mean Temperature for Whistler (°C/°F)

	Jan	Feb	Mar	Apr	May	June	July	Aug	Sept	Oct	Nov	Dec
High	−2/28	3/37	8/46	11/52	17/62	21/70	27/80	27/80	20/68	16/60	5/41	−1/30
Low	−8/18	−5/23	−3/27	2/36	7/44	9/48	11/52	11/52	8/46	3/38	−1/30	−5/23

AVERAGE SNOWFALL Expect an average snowfall of 10m (30 ft.), complemented by extensive snowmaking systems.

BEFORE YOU GO Check out the **Snow Conditions and Weather Report** from Whistler and Blackcomb mountains (✆ 604/932-4211). In Vancouver, call ✆ 604/932-4211. This lively review of ski conditions, weather, and activities on Whistler and Blackcomb mountains is updated twice daily.

For **weather and road reports,** phone the BC Ministry of Transportation Road Report Information Service (© **900/565-4997;** there's a 75¢ per minute charge) or go to **www.gov.bc.ca/tran.** For **radio** reports en route to Whistler, listen to Mountain FM Radio weather and road reports every 20 minutes starting on the hour in Squamish, 107.1 FM; Whistler, 102.1 FM; and Pemberton, 104.5 FM. Check the **www.mountainfm.com** website for a link to current road information.

In addition to the local **television** stations, The Weather Network's Road Conditions maps appear at 5 minutes to the hour and 25 minutes past the hour. Also check **www.theweathernetwork.com.**

WHISTLER CALENDAR OF EVENTS

The following information is subject to change. For exact event dates, check **www.tourismwhistler.com** or call © **800/944-7853** in the US and Canada.

JANUARY

- **FIS World Cup Freestyle**   Blackcomb Mountain showcases the world's best freestyle skiers in both aerial and mogul competitions.

FEBRUARY

- **Appleton Rum Peak to Valley Race**   Teams of four compete in Whistler Mountain's top-to-bottom ski race.
- **AltitudeX**   Popular Gay Ski Week with activities and events on Whistler and Blackcomb mountains.

MARCH

- **Couloir Extreme Race**   International extreme skiers compete on Blackcomb Mountain.

APRIL

- **Mouton Cadet Spring Festival**   Whistler Mountain hosts 2 days of individual and team ski races, including a costume competition, followed by an on-mountain picnic and barbecue each day.
- **TELUS World Ski & Snowboard Festival**   Highlights include the World Skiing Invitational and World Snowboarding Championship, outdoor concert series, action-sport photography events, demo days, film premieres, industry symposiums, and non-stop parties.
- **Whistler Cup** The world's best juvenile racers compete.

MAY

- **Master Doubles Round Robin Tournament** Whistler Racquet and Golf Resort's biggest annual tennis tournament.
- **Valley Trail 5 and 10 km (3 and 6 mile) Run** End of May.
- **Westbeach Classic** Skateboarders' Halfpipe and Skate Jam.
- **Whistler Children's Art Festival** Annual festival includes workshops on arts and crafts, plus children's entertainers, end of May.

JUNE

- **Blackcomb Mountain** Opens for summer skiing and snowboarding, mid-June.
- **Summer Solstice, World Beat Music Weekend** Features world music performances throughout Whistler Village.
- **Whistler Mountain** Last day of winter operations, mid-June.
- **Whistler Mountain** Opening day, summer operations, late June.

JULY

- **A Little Night Magic** Weekly through to September, a series of music concerts with jazz, blues, roots, world beat, retro, and family nights in outdoor village venues.
- **Canada Day Parade, July 1** Creative floats and entertainment celebrate Canada's birthday.
- **Whistler Roots Weekend** Celtic, bluegrass, world beat, and folk music performed at a free outdoor main stage.

AUGUST

- **Blackcomb Mountain** Last day of summer operations, first week in August.
- **Weetama, Whistler's Celebration of Aboriginal Culture** In the local Lil'wat Nation language, weetama is the whistling marmot after which Whistler was named. Festival showcases arts and cultures of the region's First Nations communities, ongoing in August.
- **Whistler's Really Big Street Fest** An all-star lineup of the best summer street entertainers. Performances include music, juggling, comedy, and magic.

SEPTEMBER

- **Cheakamus Challenge** A 70km (44 mile) cross-country mountain bike race featuring the best riders in Canada, including National Team members, in the longest off-road race in North America.

- **Whistler Jazz and Blues Weekend** Funky grooves, sultry sounds, blues-rockers, lounge, and gospel to Latin jazz and classic jazz vocals performed outdoors.

OCTOBER

- **Oktoberfest** Dust off your beer steins and shine those polka shoes in true European style; includes folk music and dancers, bratwurst and beer.

NOVEMBER

- **Cornucopia, Whistler's Food and Wine Celebration** Over 50 top wineries from California, Oregon, Washington, and British Columbia and an array of industry experts enjoy a weekend of gala grand tastings, winemaker dinners, food and wine seminars, and a wrap-up gourmet brunch.
- **Whistler Film Festival** A 5-day festival of ski films plus Canadian films and videos.
- **Whistler-Blackcomb Mountains Opening Day** Whistler and Blackcomb mountains kick off the ski season on the US Thanksgiving Weekend.

DECEMBER

- **Whistler WinterStart Festival** A kickoff to the ski season, with World Cup Snowboarding events, ice carving competition, and visits with Santa.
- **Breakfast with Santa at the Roundhouse Lodge** Santa joins the children on Whistler Mountain for a Christmas Eve breakfast.
- **First Night Whistler—A Family Celebration of the Arts** Whistler rings in the New Year with a participatory arts festival including music, street performers, and arts and crafts workshops, providing a family alternative to the traditional New Year's party. Alcohol strictly prohibited. Admission fees apply.
- **Nokia Snowboard FIS World Cup** The best riders in the world compete for the largest cash prizes of the World Cup circuit in North America. Competitions include freestyle halfpipe, parallel giant slalom, and snowboard-cross.

4 Top Attractions

Whistler is known for its two side-by-side mountains, **Whistler** (named after the local whistler marmot) and **Blackcomb.** The resort started out as a summer honeymoon and vacation destination then morphed into an international skiing magnet, repeatedly placing number one in North America. The original **Whistler Creekside** (the site of the first ski lift) expanded with the European-style **Whistler Village,** then multiplied to include the **Upper Village** (base of Blackcomb Mountain) and most recently **Village North** (adjacent to Whistler Village). All offer accommodations, dining, shopping, and browsing experiences. Accommodations such as townhouses and B&Bs can also be found in Whistler's residential areas, including Alta Lake Road, Bayshores, Blackcomb Benchlands, Whistler Highlands, Nordic Estates, Alta Vista, Blueberry Hill, Brio, Horstman Estates, White Gold Estates, Nesters Square, Whistler Cay, Alpine Meadows, and Emerald Estates. Outdoor activities are naturally still the main attraction. Walking, hiking, and bicycle riding are popular in summer. In winter, enjoy the snow—with everything from the obvious (all varieties of skiing) to the more obscure (snowshoeing and sleigh rides). Whistler also keeps visitors busy 12 months of the year with festivals and artistic and special events (**see "Calendar of Events,"** p. 8). To learn more about Whistler history, visit the Whistler Museum and Archives, 4329 Main St. next to the library, ✆ **604/932-2019, www.whistlermuseum. com.** Open from 10am to 4pm, Friday to Sunday in September to June; open daily in July and August.

⟨Moments First Nations Art of Renown

Most visitors are awed by the sight of Vancouver International Airport's (YVR) famed *Spirit of Haida Gwai'i, The Jade Canoe* at the entrance of the international terminal across from the food fair. Sculpted by the late Bill Reid, a famed Haida artist, the bronze sculpture stands 3.89m (12.7 ft.) high and is 6.05m (19 ft.) long. Mythical figures paddle a canoe that "goes on, forever anchored in the same place." Walk right up to this massive piece and look into the faces of Raven, The Trickster, and the Grizzly Bear who married the human female (she's in there, too).

YVR's collection of aboriginal art is of the highest quality, so you view the best. Once in Whistler, where specialty shops offer more affordable examples, you'll be better informed when buying. Two spectacularly tall, solid red cedar figures welcome international visitors in the Customs Hall. The 6m (17 ft.) *Salish Man* and *Salish Woman* are carved in early Coast Salish style by Susan A. Point, a contemporary Coast Salish artist from the Musqueam Band. The figures would have stood as house posts at the entrance of a grand longhouse. *The Spindle Whorl,* another Point carving in red cedar, sits at the top of the double escalators in the Arrivals Hall. Set against a water wall representing the Fraser River, the 5m (16 ft.) diameter work evokes a sense of flight. Two eagles, two human forms, salmon, moon, sun, and earth are symbolic of all the elements gathered at the airport location. In the US arrivals area: look for *Thunderbird* by Connie Watt, *Whaling Canoe* by Tim Paul, and *Origin of Life* by Lyle Wilson. At domestic arrivals, a collaborative work by major Haida artist Robert Davidson with Dempsey Bob and Richard Hunt is displayed. For more information, go to www.vancouverairport.com.

5 Health & Safety

Canada's health care is similar in quality to that of the United States, and while none would be refused emergency medical treatment, it's always wise to check that you have travel insurance before you leave home. If you're Canadian, make sure you have your provincial health card with you.

6 Getting to British Columbia & Whistler

BY PLANE

MAJOR AIRLINES   The Open Skies agreement between the United States and Canada has made flying to Vancouver easier than ever. There are daily direct flights between major US cities and Vancouver, your point of entry for a trip north to Whistler.

VANCOUVER INTERNATIONAL AIRPORT (YVR)   Rated one of the top 10 airports in the world by *Condé Nast Traveler* magazine, YVR is 13km (8 miles) south of downtown Vancouver on Sea Island in Richmond. More than 10 million passengers pass through YVR annually. Not surprisingly, it is something of a resort itself, with a hotel on-site, restaurants, cocktail lounges, bookstores, unisex hair salon with barber, newsstands, florists, duty-free shops, food specialty shops, ATMs, currency exchanges, a post office, and hotel reservation kiosks and phones.

Tourist Information Kiosks are located on Level 2 of the Main and International Terminals (© **604/303-3601**). Open daily from 8am to 11:30pm.

Parking is available at the airport for both loading passengers and long-term stays (© **604/276-6106**). **Courtesy buses** to the airport hotels are available. A **shuttle bus** links the Main and International Terminals to the South Terminal, where smaller and private aircraft are docked.

Fun Fact **Freshen Up**

Showers are available at **The Health Club** at The Fairmont Vancouver Airport Hotel (© **604/248-2772**). Towels and wonderfully scented toiletries, a full fitness facility, pool, and sauna are included for C$15 (US$9.35). A disposable swimsuit is C$10 (US$6.25). No baggage needed. Hotel day room rate is C$99 (US$61.85) (© **604/207-5200**). Relax or rejuvenate at two **Absolute Spa** locations in the airport: at domestic departures (© **604-273-4772**) available to all travelers, and at US departures, post-security (© **604/270-4772**). Try a 15-minute chair massage for C$20 (US$12.50) to ease the travel kinks from neck and shoulders, or an aromatherapy hydrating facial for C$60 (US$37.50), a nice treat for post-skiing skin. Full spa service includes nail repair and cosmetic touchups. You may even spot a film star at this Hollywood favorite. No appointment necessary (**www.absolutespa.com**).

DEPARTURE TAX Passengers departing Vancouver International Airport are required to purchase an Airport Improvement Fee (AIF) ticket. Children under 2 and passengers connecting through Vancouver Airport on the same day are exempt. AIF tickets must be presented along with airline tickets and boarding passes as you go through the airport security checkpoint on your way to the flight gate. The departure tax is C$15 (US$9.35) per person for international air travelers outside of North America, C$10 (US$6.25) for passengers traveling within North America (including Hawaii and Mexico), and C$5 (US$3.10) for passengers departing on flights to within BC or the Yukon.

LEAVING THE AIRPORT   The pale-green **YVR Airporter** (© **604/946-8866**) provides **airport bus service** to downtown Vancouver's major hotels. It leaves from Level 2 of the Main Terminal every 15 minutes daily from 6:30am to 10:30pm, with a final run at 12:10am. The one-way fare is C$12 (US$7.50) for adults, C$9 (US$5.60) for seniors, and C$5 (US$3.10) for children; the round-trip fare is C$18 (US$11.25) for adults, C$17 (US$10.60) for seniors, and C$10 (US$6.25) for children. Bus service back to the airport leaves from selected downtown hotels every half-hour between 5:35am and 10:55pm. Scheduled pickups serve the bus station at Main and Terminal avenues, Hotel Vancouver, Waterfront Centre Hotel, Georgian Court, Sutton Place, Landmark, and others.

BY CAR

Most major **car rental firms** have airport counters and shuttles. Make advance reservations for fast check-in and guaranteed availability, especially if you want a four-wheel-drive vehicle. Whistler is a 2-hour drive north of Vancouver on Highway 99 but may take longer if you encounter traffic congestion crossing Vancouver or snowy weather conditions en route.

Tourists are permitted to drive in BC for up to 6 months if they hold a valid driver's license from another province, state, or country, or for up to 12 months if they also hold an International Driver's Permit issued outside of Canada.

Drivers from the Vancouver International Airport to Whistler must pass through downtown Vancouver. Consult a city map before setting out, as the route is complicated by a multitude of bridges crossing the Fraser River and the Narrows to North Vancouver by way of the Lions Gate Bridge or the Ironworkers Memorial Second Narrows Bridge.

Highway 99 is known locally as the Sea to Sky Highway, and the trip is a spectacular climb from sea level to Whistler Village at 675m (2,214 ft.). It's a tricky drive, so take it easy. Highway 99 requires caution, especially when it rains or snows. The road twists alongside cliffs and canyons and is extremely narrow in several places. In winter, it is highly recommended that you have suitable snow/winter tires. If you have all-weather tires, bring chains and know how to install them. Heavy snowfalls do happen and a shovel and road salt may be required.

Having driven to Whistler in every kind of weather, I advise driving during daylight hours. Definitely follow the speed limit of 80km

(50 miles) per hour unless otherwise posted. Don't be pressured by drivers lurking behind you, as there are 10 passing lanes along the route. (You'll have the last laugh when you see the speeders pulled over for a hefty ticket.) For safety's sake, leave your headlights on at all times. The use of safety belts, child restraints, bicycle helmets, and motorcycle helmets is mandatory in British Columbia.

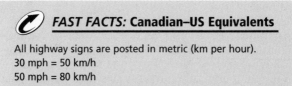

> ### *FAST FACTS:* Canadian–US Equivalents
>
> All highway signs are posted in metric (km per hour).
> 30 mph = 50 km/h
> 50 mph = 80 km/h
>
> 1km equals 5/8 or .621 miles
> 1 mile equals 1⅔ or 1.6km
>
> Gasoline is sold in liters.
> 3.78 liters = 1 US gallon

LIMOUSINE AND VAN SERVICE

Looking in the Whistler phone book, you'd think everyone came up by limousine, as more than a dozen limo services are listed. Among them are **Star Limousine Service,** offering a fleet of late-model limos and passenger vans departing from Vancouver International Airport. Each luxury car is chauffeured by a seasoned and experienced driver. Vans can carry 10 passengers plus ski equipment. All vans come with ski/snowboard box. A stretch limo (seats six) costs C$300 (US$187.50) one-way; a super-stretch limo (seats 10) is C$400 (US$250) one-way. A posh executive van, complete with sound system and chauffeur, is C$325 (US$203) one-way. To book, call ✆ **800/803-9222.** During the ski season, **Whistler Star Express** vans, mini-buses, and limousines offer door-to-door shuttle service, with complimentary ski racks and child seats. Adults C$55 (US$34.35); children under 11 years old C$30 (US$18.75). For reservations call ✆ **604/685-5546,** or the Whistler local line ✆ **604/905-7668.**

BY BUS

Bus is a popular way to get to Whistler, especially in winter when a car isn't really needed to get around. **Perimeter Whistler Express** offers nine daily departures in winter (varies in summer) between international and domestic terminals at Vancouver International Airport and Whistler, and can stop at 23 different Vancouver hotels. Travel time is 2.5 hours depending on road and traffic conditions. Fares include taxes. Adult (12+) C$58.85 (US$36.80) one-way; return C$117.70 (US$73.55). Children aged 5 to 11 (4 and under free) one-way C$36.40 (US$22.75); return C$72.75 (US$45.45). Call © **604/266-5386** or go to **www.perimeterbus.com.**

Greyhound Canada   Seven round-trip buses per day to Whistler Village bus loop from Pacific Central station at 1150 Station St. (Main Street and Terminal Avenue) in downtown Vancouver (© **604/482-8747**). The bus leaves from the Whistler Bus Depot, 4338 Main St., Village North (© **604/932-5031**). Travel time is 2.5 hours. Special fares may be subject to restrictions. All fares include taxes. Adult fare is C$20 (US$12.50) one-way; round-trip C$40 (US$25). Senior fare (65 years and older) is C$18 (US$11.25) one-way; round-trip C$36 (US$22.50). Children 5 to 11 years when traveling with an adult (4 and under free) C$10 (US$6.25) one-way; round-trip C$20 (US$12.50). Check with an agent for schedules or go to **www.greyhound.ca.**

BY TRAIN

For a luxury trip at an affordable price, take **BC Rail** from the North Vancouver train station at 1311 West 1st St., a taxi ride over the spectacular Lions Gate Bridge. Trains leave daily at 7am. Enjoy a full breakfast northbound along with splendid views of Howe Sound as you hug the shoreline. Southbound, you'll be served a full dinner at your seat. Disembark at 10am at Whistler Creekside. A free shuttle takes you to and from the Whistler Gateway bus loop. Prices are seasonal, and there are also seat sales during various periods. The regular-rate one-way trip to Whistler is C$39 (US$24.35); same-day return is C$69 (US$43.10). Children 2 to 12 years C$23 (US14.35) one-way; C$44 (US$27.50) round-trip. In British Columbia, call © **800/339-8752;** outside BC and in the US call © **800/663-8238;** and in Vancouver area call © **604/984-5246, www.bcrail.com.**

2

Getting to Know Whistler

Oldtimers in Whistler like to recall "the early days" around 1966 when the Red Chair gondola and two T-bars at Whistler Creekside officially opened. It was a wide-open place back then, some say even lawless. Residents lived a hippie lifestyle in makeshift cabins, coming out only to ski or party. It's not like that anymore. Whistler today has 115 hotels, condos, and bed and breakfasts, offering more than 5,334 rooms. On any given winter day, Whistler's resident population of 9,000 swells to 40,000 visitors. Summer and winter, they swarm the more than 93 restaurants, lounges, and bars, 207 retail shops, and three golf courses. Whistler Resort has all the services you could want, including banking, foreign exchange and bank machines, church services, medical and dental clinics, physiotherapy and massage therapy, office services, a public library, museum, movie theater and video rentals, health and fitness centers, public swimming pool, ice rink, indoor tennis courts, spa facilities, and beauty salons.

You can't stop progress—and the old truism is especially apt in Whistler, where progress (as in growth and development) has happened at the speed of light. The Resort Municipality of Whistler was founded in 1975. In 1976 an official community plan was introduced and Whistler Village began to take shape. Blackcomb Mountain opened in 1980, doubling the area's ski capacity, and the Upper Village was developed. By 1995 Village North was launched, and is now a fully developed addition to the resort picture.

The Resort Municipality of Whistler even has its sights on the 2010 Winter Olympics—and not for the first time. Truth is, the first lift back in 1966 came with the same dream. The first time around, that dream wasn't realized. The Vancouver-Whistler 2010 Olympic bid comes with a lot more credibility.

Whistler today is more than skiing and partying, although these two activities rate high on the agenda. So many choices abound in such a small area that it would be difficult to run out of options. Are you the laidback type, best suited for lolling on the beach at Alta Lake, or the cultural type, taking in a classical concert? Perhaps you'd rather rent a mountain bike and tackle the Cheakamus Canyon or golf on a pro-designed course? Everyone knows that skiing and snowboarding are the main winter sports, but what about an old-fashioned sleigh ride or an evening stroll through Whistler, admiring the sparkling holiday lights that seem to bedeck every tree and building? Activities these days may not be lawless, but they're never boring.

1 Orientation

Before you know it, you'll be buzzing around Whistler as if you lived there. The resort stretches along the Whistler Valley. As you enter, you'll pass Function Junction on the left, then Whistler Creekside on the right. From here it's 4km (2.5 miles) to the Whistler Village sign. Turn right here on to Village Gate Boulevard. Whistler Village is on the right and Village North on the left. Straight ahead is the free day-parking lot; Whistler and Blackcomb mountains are side by side, with Whistler Mountain on the right. Turn right at Blackcomb Way for the Upper Village, with the Fairmont Chateau Whistler as the crown jewel of Blackcomb Mountain.

⟲ Welcome to the Old Days

Before the mid-1800s, local First Nations tribes traveled on what became known as the Pemberton Trail. Gold seekers followed the same route during the Gold Rush that started in 1859. By 1888, the first permanent European settlers established homes in the Brackendale area. In 1914 Whistler's most renowned couple, Alex and Myrtle Philip, built Rainbow Lodge on Alta Lake, and by the 1930s were hosts at the premier summer resort west of Banff. In 1966, when the Garibaldi Lift Company opened the first lift, the name of London Mountain was changed to Whistler Mountain and a new era was born.

For more on local First Nations people, fauna and flora, and memorable Myrtle, visit the **Whistler Museum & Archives** at 4329 Main St., Village North, next door to the Whistler Public Library (© 604/932-2019; www.whistler museum.org). Open daily from 10am to 4pm in summer; Thursday to Sunday September to June. Admission is C$2 (US$1.25).

Whistler Valley

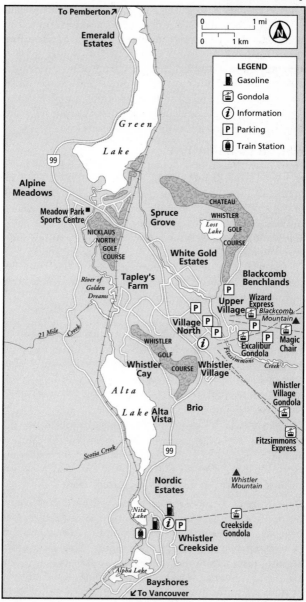

To Pemberton ↗

Emerald Estates

0 — 1 mi
0 — 1 km
N

LEGEND
- Gasoline
- Gondola
- *i* Information
- P Parking
- Train Station

Green Lake

99

Alpine Meadows

Meadow Park Sports Centre ■

NICKLAUS NORTH GOLF COURSE

Spruce Grove

CHATEAU
WHISTLER
GOLF
Lost Lake
COURSE

White Gold Estates

Blackcomb Benchlands

River of Golden Dreams

Tapley's Farm

P Upper Village Wizard Express

P Village North *Blackcomb Mountain* ▲

21 Mile Creek

P P Excalibur Gondola P Magic Chair

i

WHISTLER GOLF COURSE

Fitzsimmons Creek

Whistler Cay

Whistler Village

Alta Lake

Alta Vista

Brio

Whistler Village Gondola

Fitzsimmons Express

Scotia Creek

99

Nordic Estates

Whistler Mountain ▲

Nita Lake

i P

Whistler Creekside

Creekside Gondola

Alpha Lake

Bayshores
↙ To Vancouver

If you continue driving along Highway 99 you'll come to more residential areas, with condo rentals and bed and breakfast accommodations, Nesters Market (a small mall), and the **Meadow Park Sports Centre** 6km (4 miles) north of Whistler Village (© **604/ 935-7529**). If your children like to swim, the pool is a magical place with features such as a lazy river, a vortex, and spouting bears. Twenty-three km (14 miles) north is Pemberton, a small town that now acts as a bedroom community for Whistler workers and makes for a pleasant day trip farther into the mountains.

VISITOR INFORMATION

The Whistler Visitor Info Center, 2097 Lake Placid Rd., Whistler, BC V0N 1B0 (© **604/932-5528**), is open daily from 9am to 5pm. **Information kiosks** on Village Gate Boulevard at the entry to Whistler Village, the main bus stop, and a number of other locations are open from mid-May to early September during the same hours. **Tourism Whistler** at the Whistler Conference Center, 4010 Whistler Way, Whistler, BC V0N 1B0, is open daily from 9am to 5pm (© **604/932-3928; www.tourismwhistler.com**). This office can assist you with event tickets and last-minute accommodations bookings, as well as provide general information.

WHISTLER LAYOUT

The Resort Municipality of Whistler is the culmination of a dream that began in the 1970s with a conscious decision to build a resort town. Planners looked into their crystal balls and predicted a resort town of 40,000 beds, arranged around a central village. Whistler is nearing full capacity, with the original Whistler Village joined by several new developments.

Whistler Village   Compact and car-free (park in the nearby free parking lot or pay for parking in hotel lots), Whistler Village is located at the base of both Whistler and Blackcomb mountains. Pedestrians can explore the Village Stroll and its many nooks and crannies, with frequent stops for shopping and dining.

Upper Village   Wrapped around the base of Blackcomb Mountain, the area includes Blackcomb lifts, hotels, restaurants, pubs, and shopping. The Intrawest Corporation opened Blackcomb Mountain in 1980. Intrawest is still busy in the Upper Village, joining Four Seasons Hotels and Resorts to develop the Four Seasons Resort Whistler, a 273-room luxury property opening in the spring of 2004. It will be the first Four Seasons resort sold to individuals as condominiums and then managed as a full-service hotel.

> ### ⓘ Tips   Meet the Locals at Function Junction
>
> Function Junction is the clever name given to this industrial annex south of Whistler Village. It's home to retail and industrial businesses, including WAVE (Whistler's public transit bus system), a building center, equipment rentals, an automotive service center, a hardware store, framers, furniture repairers, and more. Several cafes, coffee shops, and catering outlets let you experience a down-to-earth side of Whistler.

Village North   What is now a fully developed second village started life as a huge unpaved parking lot across from Whistler Village. During the mud months of May and November it was only the desperate who parked there, including at least one now–upstanding member of the Whistler restaurant scene who started his life there living in his van in said parking lot.

Village North now includes wide, pedestrian-only promenades and specific retail areas, such as Whistler Town Plaza and Whistler Marketplace.

Whistler Creekside   Called the "home of the downhill," Creekside does have a real creek running through it. Nearby is Whistler Mountain's Creekside Gondola base. Left behind for a time by Whistler Village development, Creekside is catching up with Intrawest Resort Development Group's C$50-million (US$31-million) revitalization, including the newly opened Legends condo-hotel. Following will be Tracks lodge in the fall of 2002. Like Legends, it is a whole-ownership condo-hotel. The first phase of Franz's Trail, a new retail walkway, is now open and by winter 2003 will include boutique-style retail shops, a coffee shop, and a grocery store.

☎ Useful Telephone Numbers

Emergency
Ambulance, Fire, Royal Canadian Mounted Police ☎ **911**

Alcoholic Beverages
Marketplace Liquor Store ☎ **604/932-7251**

Banks/Automated Teller Machines (ATM)/Currency Exchange
Custom House Currency Exchange (three locations in
Whistler Village) ☎ **604/938-0858;** ☎ **604/938-1051;**

ⓒ **604/938-6658.** Express Cash Teller ATM (located in Upper Village, base of Blackcomb Mountain). North Shore Credit Union (located in Whistler Village) ⓒ **888/713-6777.**

Royal Bank of Canada and ATM (located in Whistler Village) ⓒ **604/938-5800.** Royal Bank of Canada ATM (located in Whistler Village, Mountain Square).

TD Bank and ATM (located in Village North) ⓒ **604/905-5500.** TD Bank ATM (two ATMS at Mountain Square and Skier's Plaza)

Dentists
Dr. James McKenzie ⓒ **604/932-3677**
Dr. John Roberts ⓒ **604/938-1550**

Eye Care
Whistler Eye Clinic ⓒ **604/932-2600**

Groceries
Food Plus ⓒ **604/932-6193**
The Grocery Store ⓒ **604/932-3628**
IGA Plus ⓒ **604/938-2850**
Nesters Market ⓒ **604/932-3545**

Library
Whistler Public Library ⓒ **604/932-5564**

Medical Services
Creekside Medical Clinic ⓒ **604/932-4404**
Town Plaza Medical Clinic, Whistler Marketplace in Village North (offers walk-in service) ⓒ **604/905-7089**
Whistler Health Care Center, 4380 Lorimer Rd. (physicians and emergency service as well as lab and X-ray facilities available) ⓒ **604/932-4911**
Village Center Chiropractic and Massage ⓒ **604/932-2111**
Whistler Physiotherapy I (Whistler Marketplace) ⓒ **604/932-4001,** II (Creekside) ⓒ **604/938-9001**
(For spas, massage, and health clubs, see chapter 7, "Shopping from A to Z")

Office Services
Jody's Internet Services ⓒ **604/932-8380**
Whistler Office Services ⓒ **604-932-5114**

Pet Services/Veterinarian
Coast Mountain Veterinary Services ⓒ **604/932-5391**
Puppy Zone Day Care ⓒ **604/905-6705**

Pharmacies

Pharmasave (Whistler Village in Village Square)
℃ **604/932-2303**, (Village North in Whistler Marketplace)
℃ **604/932-4251**

Postal/Courier Services

Canada Post Office ℃ **604/932-5012**
Mail Boxes Etc. ℃ **604/932-6236**

Real Estate Companies/Mortgage Brokers

There comes a moment in every visitor's life when they think
it would be great to buy a place at Whistler. And there's a
pack of Realtors just waiting to talk to you.
Garibaldi Mortgage ℃ **604/905-3800**
Re/Max of Whistler ℃ **604/932-2300**
Sussex Realty ℃ **604/932-3006**
Whistler Real Estate Company ℃ **604/932-5538**
Windermere Sea to Sky Real Estate ℃ **604/932-4117**

Religious Services

Gateway to the Mountains (Jewish faith) ℃ **604/935-8452**
Maurice Young Millennium Place (Interfaith) ℃ **604/905-4211**
Our Lady of the Mountains Catholic Church ℃ **604/905-4781**
Whistler Community Church/Meeting Place ℃ **604/932-3139**
Whistler United Church ℃ **604/932-5104**
Whistler Village Church (Multi-faith) ℃ **604/935-3735**

Resort Municipality of Whistler ℃ **604/932-5535**

Travel Agent

Thomas Cook Marlin Travel ℃ **800/252-8232**, ℃ **604/938-0111**

2 Getting Around

Much of Whistler, including Whistler Village, Upper Village, and
Village North, is compact and pedestrian-oriented. If you're staying
for the day, park your car in the free day-parking lot and leave it. The
walk between Whistler Village (Whistler Mountain) and Upper
Village (Blackcomb Mountain) is a short 5 minutes. Village North is
across the road from Whistler Village.

BY BUS   WAVE, the Whistler public transit system (℃ **604/932-
4020**), was launched December 1, 1991, with five buses and
325,000 riders in its first year. Year 2000 ridership was an amazing
2,270,000 on a fleet of 24 buses. Whistler has the highest per capita
transit ridership in the province, and has been a leader in technology

with its introduction of magnetic swipe cards for prepaid fares. A year-round service, WAVE operates frequently from the Tamarisk district and the BC Rail Station to the neighboring districts of Nesters Village, Alpine Meadows, and Emerald Estates. Bus service from Whistler Village to Village North and the Upper Village is free. For other routes, one-way fares are C$1.50 (US$.95) for adults and C$1.25 (US$.75) for seniors/students. Children under 5 are free.

Tips Goodies to Your Door

Resort Room Service is a neat idea that lets you kick back in your hotel room while someone else goes out to pick up your groceries or liquor. Grocery delivery is C$8.95 (US$5.60) on orders up to eight items from IGA, Whistler's largest grocery store (charges vary on larger orders). Liquor, cold beer, and wine is C$8.95 (US$5.60) for anything up to C$90 (US$56.25). If more, add 15% charge to bill. ℭ **604/905-4711.**

BY TAXI   Whistler Taxi, Sea To Sky Taxi, and Blackcomb Taxi (ℭ **604/932-3333, 604/938-3333**) operate around the clock. They make deliveries, provide service to and from Vancouver and Pemberton Airport, and offer sightseeing tours, VIP service, and luxury passenger vans and luxury sedans.

BY CAR   Avis Rent-a-Car (ℭ **604/932-1236;** aviswhistler@telus.net) is located in the lobby of the Holiday Inn Sunspree at the corner of Village Gate Boulevard and Blackcomb Way. Courtesy pick-up available.

✐ FAST FACTS: They All Love Whistler

Whistler boasted a 124% increase in revenues in the 1999–2000 season. Look around you at the lift—you may see Arnold Schwarzenegger and other movie stars shoulder to shoulder. These are the folks who can afford the increasing number of C$1-million-plus ski homes that are being built here, their preferred choice of accommodations. Whether they rent or buy, they appreciate the privacy.

Studies show that the majority of winter visitors are single males, aged 22 to 44, with annual earnings of C$50,000 to C$75,000. They stay 5 nights on average, easily dropping a couple of thousand dollars for their ski break.

3

Where to Stay

For such a small place, Whistler Resort has some very fine accommodations. Standards are high, based on intense competition for business. Many hotels have received awards and commendations for excellence. Two made it into *Condé Nast Traveler*'s 2001 reader's survey of the Top 30 Resort Properties in North America. Westin Resort & Spa placed 14th on the list and Fairmont Chateau Whistler was 18th.

With more than 24,000 "rental pillows" in Whistler Valley, finding a place to stay is not difficult, but you must book ahead, especially for the busy Christmas/New Year's period. **Whistler Central Reservations** (4010 Whistler Way, Whistler, BC V0N 1B4, ✆ **800/ WHISTLER** or 604/932-2394, fax 604/932-3928 or 932-7231, www.tourismwhistler.com) has more than 2,000 rental units on its roster, including standard hotel rooms, condominium-style suites, and B&Bs. They can also provide a customized package with lift tickets and air or ground transportation to and from Vancouver.

Property managers such as **Whistler Lodging Company,** which represents 1,000 units, making it the largest property manager in Whistler (✆ **604/800/777-0185,** fax 604/633-2948, www.whistler lodgingco.com), and **ResortQuest** with over 600 units in Whistler (✆ **888/830-7031** or 604/932-6699, fax 604/932-6622, www. resortquestwhistler.com), can help you choose and make reservations that suit all budgets and group sizes. Call them directly, or book through Whistler Central Reservations. Checking the websites is very helpful, with photos of properties and individual rooms.

Your first decision is whether to stay in Whistler Village or farther afield. In the car-free Village you can walk everywhere. The cobblestone streets are lively with visitors on their way to lifts, shopping, or dining. But if you're looking for a quiet place to stay, you have to shop around in the Village. Ask for a room away from the pedestrian strolls.

If you stay in Village North, in the Upper Village by the Blackcomb lifts, or farther afield in Whistler Creekside or elsewhere, you'll have a better chance of getting a quiet spot. On the other hand, if you stay outside the Village you may have to drive, take a taxi, or bus.

Whistler offers a dizzying array of places to stay, including hotel rooms, condos, lodges, townhomes, vacation homes, bed and breakfasts, and rock-bottom accommodations. Where you end up depends on the activities you want to pursue, your group's size, and your budget. The various booking agencies can help you determine the best choice. A C$3,000 (US$1,875) a night vacation home might be a better bet in some cases, depending on circumstances. I met a group of seven doctors from a Midwest US city who all pitched in to share such a home, and raved about the two hot tubs and secluded but convenient location.

In winter (with the exception of the pricey 10 days from pre-Christmas to New Year's) you can stay in Whistler for prices that range from a moderate under-C$200 per night (US$125), to expensive (between C$200 and C$300 per night [US$125 to US$187.50]), and very expensive (over C$300 per night [US$187.50]). There are also some basic, budget accommodations at under C$100 per night (US$62.50) or less. Try to make reservations by September for the Christmas season, as well as February and March. In summer (May to October), rates drop temptingly. July and August are the busiest months, and have the highest rates.

If you check the websites noted you may find some good deals offered, both winter and summer. Hotels often advertise packages or specials, such as stay for 3 nights, pay for 2. Don't be afraid to ask if you call.

1 Hotels

VERY EXPENSIVE

Club Intrawest &&   Owned by Intrawest, the company that owns and runs Whistler and Blackcomb mountains, Club Intrawest is the prize for people who purchase a pricey membership and pay a yearly fee. That said, the lodge-style accommodation does have some suites open to non-members. Luxurious and well-appointed, they have full kitchens, high-end appliances and fixtures, and ample-sized rooms. A nice touch is Canadian art and sculpture on the walls and elsewhere. Some rooms come with extras like a giant in-suite Jacuzzi just off the bedroom, great for sybaritic nights. Then there are the club facilities, which you get to use even if you're a non-member. These are easily the best in Whistler, with two swimming pools, three hot tubs, an 18m (60 ft.) waterslide, a steam room that's actually hot, a big-screen TV room, an in-house movie theater, a library, and more. Located a very short walk to Blackcomb's ski lifts, across from the Fairmont Chateau Whistler, Club Intrawest is well-positioned for both winter and summer stays.

4580 Chateau Blvd., Whistler, BC V0N 1B4. *€* 877/258-6362 or 604/938-3030. Fax 604/938-9281. www.clubintrawest.com. 200 units. Winter: C$391 (US$244.35) 1 bedroom; C$1,224 (US$765) 3 bedroom. Summer: C$252 (US$157.50) 1-bedroom vacation home; C$729 (US$455.60) 3-bedroom vacation home. AE, MC, V. Parking C$14 (US$8.75). **Amenities:** Grocery store, ski/bike storage, 2 pools, gym, spa, 3 hot tubs, electronic games room for children, movie room showing 3 fairly current movies per day, concierge. *In room:* Laundry (in 1-bedroom and up), TV/VCR, hair dryer.

Delta Whistler Resort 🐾🐾   Steps away from the Whistler and Blackcomb gondolas and the bustle of Whistler Village, the newly renovated hotel offers spacious rooms, big beds, and spectacular mountain views. You're greeted at the door, and your luggage is picked up and delivered to your room. Different room configurations can be assembled from the 288 units available. Double Jacuzzi tubs come with Premier Rooms; a dry sauna is yours in one of six Executive Suites. A fireplace crackles in the bedroom of the 151 sq. m (1,632 sq. ft.) Mountain Suite; there's a dry sauna too, plus you can add two adjoining bedrooms. The Health Club, on the main floor off the lobby, is spacious and has a generous supply of towels. The staff are very accommodating. The heated outdoor pool and hot tub have a great view of the mountains. The full-service Mountain Spa offers massage and shiatsu therapy and up-to-date exercise equipment.

4050 Whistler Way, Whistler, BC V0N 1B4. *€* **888/244-8666** or *€* 604/932-1982. Fax 604/932-7332. www.deltawhistler.com. 288 units. Winter: C$299 (US$186.85) hotel, C$349 (US$218) studio deluxe. Summer: C$189 (US$118) hotel, C$209 (US$130.60) studio deluxe. Parking C$18 (US$11.25). AE, DC, DISC, MC, V. **Amenities:** Wheelchair accessible, lounge, restaurant, pool, spa, hot tub, concierge. The Delta Resort is pet-friendly. *In room:* A/C, satellite TV/VCR, minibar, bathrobes, Nintendo, voice mail, data jacks, a safe for valuables.

🖊 Tips on Accommodations

Add a 17% tax (7% GST, 10% hotel tax) to accommodations, which may be partially refundable to US visitors. Parking fees vary from free to C$22 (US$13.75) a night, and are lower in summer. Telephone charges also vary, from free to a per-call charge. Ask about cancellation policies. Once you've booked, you may be charged if you change even a small detail. And if you have to cancel your booking, you may lose a sizable chunk of your deposit, or may be charged for at least one night.

Most accommodations have at least some rooms that are wheelchair accessible.

All winter and summer rates quoted are a range of Value Season "base" prices according to Tourism Whistler Central Reservations in 2001. Prices and availability will vary greatly, and rates in most cases will have increased by the summer of 2002. Rates for the peak Christmas–New Year's season will be substantially higher.

Rates listed here are based on double occupancy. Ask about extra charges if you're bringing more people. Children can usually stay free with parents or guardians. Sometimes the cut-off age is 18, sometimes it's younger. A charge of between C$20 and C$35 (US$12.50 to US$21.85) per night is applied for extra adults.

All rooms come with a coffeemaker unless noted in the review. All swimming pools in Whistler are heated and outdoors, unless otherwise noted.

Ask about check-in and check-out times. For most places it's 4pm, but for some it's 3pm. Likewise, most will want you out by 10am, while others let you stay until 11am (which I certainly feel is more civilized).

The number of units noted is the number of units available for rental, not the total number of units in the accommodation.

The Fairmont Chateau Whistler *☆☆☆*   *Ski Magazine* rates the Fairmont Chateau Whistler one of the top 10 ski resort hotels in the world. In a word, this hotel is impressive, and a longtime favorite. The Chateau echoes the finest of Rocky Mountain retreats. As soon as you enter the massive lobby filled with rich carpets and Canadian art you definitely feel like a person of importance, yet quite at ease. The rooms and suites feature double queen- and king-size beds, duvets, robes, and soaker tubs. This year the Chateau is even better, with the million-dollar renovation of The Wildflower restaurant, featuring a private wine room, no less, for the true wine connoisseur. Ski-in ski-out Blackcomb Mountain, with civilized après-ski drinks in The Mallard Bar, an impressive example of the Chateau-style decor. You may spot a Hollywood star; Pierce Brosnan, Sean Penn, and Arnold Schwarzenegger are just a few of the celebrated guests. A Fairmont hotel, the Chateau is luxurious, but good deals can be ferreted out, especially during off-peak, "shoulder" times. Go to the website or call direct. Located in the Upper Village, it's a quick walk past Rebagliatti Park (named after the local gold medal Olympic snowboarder) to Whistler Village.

4599 Chateau Blvd., Whistler, BC V0N 1B4. ⓒ **800/441-1414,** in-house reservations ⓒ **800/606-8244** or 604/938-8000. Fax 604/938-2291. www.fairmont.com. 558 units. Winter: C$329 (US$205.60) standard, C$529 (US$330.60) premier. Summer: C$219 (US$136.85) standard, C$369 (US$230.60) premier. AE, DC, DISC, MC, V. Self parking C$20 (US$12.50), underground valet parking C$25 (US$15.60). **Amenities:** Wheelchair accessible. Room service, concierge, ski and bike storage, pool, full-service spa, massage therapy, sauna, whirlpool, steam room, weight room, terrace barbecue, tennis courts, 18-hole golf course. *In room:* A/C, TV/VCR, minibar, hair dryer.

Le Chamois ⓕ The feel here is European, not mountain lodge. This is an older hotel built way back in 1990 (Whistler time), before European styling was pre-empted by mountain lodge decor. The suites look very pared down after all the timber and plaids of the majority of hotels in Whistler, so don't stay here if you're looking for lodge decor. On the other hand, they are somewhat larger than most other accommodations. Studio suites have gigantic in-room Jacuzzis with views of Rainbow and Sproat mountains. Studio up to decorator-designed four-bedroom suites are available, with queen or king beds depending on size of suite. Efficiency kitchens are in studio and one-bedroom suites, and full kitchens in others. The efficiency units are not recommended for families. **Summit Service** is available to guests and provides daily turndown service, newspaper, upgraded amenities, and luxury bathrobes. The **Resort Xtras Program** is available for a daily extra fee of C$7 (US$4.35), or C$25 (US$15.60) for your stay. With it, you get complimentary local calls, daily video rentals, in-room coffee, newspaper, incoming faxes, laundry soap, Internet access plus a complimentary phone card with $5 free long-distance, a pass to the Meadow Park Sports Centre for all room occupants, and more. The lobby is intimate, with a small seating area with fireplace by the Cigar Company Ltd. boutique and three good restaurants on the premises. Located at the base of the Wizard Express on Blackcomb Mountain, this is a ski-in/ski-out facility.

4557 Blackcomb Way, Whistler, BC V0N 1B0. ⓒ **800/777-0185** or 604/932-8700. Fax 604/905-2576. www.whistler-lechamois.com. 48 units. Winter: C$329 (US$205.60) 1 bedroom, C$529 (US$330.60) 2 bedroom. Summer: C$149–C$240

(US$93–US$150) 1 bedroom, C$330 (US$206.25) 2 bedroom. Parking C$8–C$12 (US$5–US$7.50). AE, MC, V. **Amenities:** Wheelchair accessible. Ski/bike storage, small lap pool, hot tub, exercise facility, 24-hr. front desk. Room service for breakfast and dinner. Intimate studios with large in-room Jacuzzi tubs. *In room:* A/C, TV/VCR, hair dryer, efficiency or full kitchens.

The Pan Pacific Lodge 👣👣👣   You can't get closer to the Village's high-speed gondolas than The Pan Pacific Lodge. In less than a minute, you're up and away for a day of skiing or mountain exploration. Or you can simply relax at poolside or in the hot tub, with a ringside seat on the mountains. The hotel is on the small side, and rooms go quickly, so reserve well in advance. Studio and one- and two-bedroom units are spacious and well-appointed, with a Craftsman twist on the decor that makes the rooms look sleeker than most. All suites have kitchens, providing everything to cook up a gourmet meal. With sofa beds and fold-down Murphy beds, the studio suites are fine for couples, while the one- and two-bedroom suites allow more space for larger groups or families with kids. One interesting twist to hotel service is the Dream Room concept. On a second honeymoon ask for Dean to deck out your bedroom as the Night of 1,000 Stars, with Arabian-style draperies and your bed covered in rose petals. Cost for the special effect is around C$2,500 (US$1562.50). The Canadian Romance decor, complete with four-poster bed, is C$1,000 (US$625) or so. They treat you right here. "The Pan" assigns a staff member to take care of you throughout your stay, carrying your bags, answering your questions, and so on. To get to your room, you have to pass by the 24-hour concierge at the front desk, an excellent security feature.

4320 Sundial Crescent, Whistler, BC V0N 1B4. © 888/905-9995 or 604/905-2999. Fax 604/905-2995. www.panpac.com. 121 units. Winter: C$359 (US$224.35) 1-bedroom suite, C$559 (US$349.35) 2-bedroom suite. Summer: C$179 (US$111.85) 1-bedroom suite, C$229 (US$143) 2-bedroom suite. Parking C$16 (US$10). AE, DC, MC, V. **Amenities:** Wheelchair accessible. Ski/bike/golf storage, room service; concierge; laundry; heated outdoor pool, hot tubs; fitness center, steam room. *In room:* Fully equipped kitchen, soaker tub, salon amenities from Aveda, plush robes, in-room safes, Internet access, on-command video, 2-line phones.

Residence Inn at Marriott   Located high on Blackcomb Mountain for ski-in/ski-out convenience, the inn is surrounded by forest and spectacular views. This is the ultimate ski-in/ski-out location. Ski from the lobby down to the lifts, then ski back in when you're finished your run. Large rooms with fireplaces and fully equipped kitchens, back rooms facing the forest, and outdoor pool and hot tubs carved out of the mountainside all contribute to an enjoyable stay. A free shuttle bus to and from the village runs every 10 minutes from the front door. Generous with in-suite towels, and pool towels are available at the front desk. The free breakfast buffet is a fun place to meet other guests. Make your own waffles using little cups of waffle batter and a real waffle iron. Add from fresh fruit, yogurt, cereal, and baskets of baked goods. The fitness facilities are excellent, and popular with guests. On the downside, I could do without the drunken men with their case of beer who just wouldn't leave the outdoor hot tub. No one seemed to monitor the facility, even though it was just outside the main lobby area. Summit Service and Resort Xtras Program are available (see Le Chamois for details).

4899 Painted Cliff Rd., Whistler, BC V0N 1B4. ℂ **800/777-0185** or 604/905-3400. Fax 604/905-3432. www.residenceinn.com and www.whistlerlodgingco.com. 186 units. Winter: C$359 (US$224) 1 bedroom, C$559 (US$349.35) 2 bedrooms. Summer: C$260 (US$162.50) 1 bedroom, C$340 (US$212.50) 2 bedrooms. Parking C$12 (US$7.50) per night in winter, C$8 (US$5) per night in summer. Pet-friendly; C$20 (US$12.50) nightly per pet. AE, DC, MC, V. **Amenities:** Common laundry rooms; ski/bike storage. Checkout is 11am. After you check out, luggage can be stored on-site, and the spa facilities used to freshen up after your ski or hike. Pool, hot tubs, fitness facilities. Complimentary continental breakfast daily. *In room:* Full kitchens, TV/VCR, hair dryer.

The Westin Resort & Spa Whistler 🏵🏵🏵

If the staff weren't so friendly, The Westin Resort & Spa Whistler might be intimidating to mere common mortals. The parking attendant whisks your car to some mysterious underground parking area, a doorman piles your bags onto a cart, and you waltz into the huge lobby to check in unencumbered by the mundane chores of normal life. This luxury all-suite hotel, which opened in April 2000, pulls out all the stops to make visitors feel pampered. If you're skiing, they warm your boots and get your skis ready for you. If you have children, the Whistler Kids Club program will keep them occupied while you enjoy a few hours in the Avello Spa or a drink at the FireRock Lounge before dinner at the exceptional Aubergine Grille. All accommodations are condo-style suites, from one-bedroom to mountain suites (sleeping six). Each has a full kitchen, dining area, and living room. Having a well-appointed kitchen, with microwave, full-size fridge, and kitchenware makes it easy to stay in and cook, a nice touch if visiting with children. Add The Westin's famously comfortable Heavenly Bed, and views of the mountains for a memorable stay.

4090 Whistler Way, Whistler, BC V0N 1B4. ℂ **800/634-5577**, 604/905-5000. Fax 604/905-5589. www.westinwhistler.net. 419 units. Winter: C$369 (US$230.60) 1 bedroom, C$529 (US$330.60) 2 bedrooms. Summer: C$199 (US$124.37) 1 bedroom, C$349 (US$218) 2 bedrooms. Children 18 and under stay free. Extra adult

C$30 (US$18.75). Valet or self parking C$21(US$13) per night in winter; C$16 (US$10) per night in summer. AE, DC, DISC, MC, V. **Amenities:** Wheelchair accessible. Ski valet and complimentary shuttle to local golf courses, spa and health club, ski and bike storage, outdoor and indoor pools, fitness center, spa, 2 Jacuzzis, children's club, concierge, dry cleaning, laundry on each floor. *In room:* Refreshment basket, full kitchen, soaker tub, down duvet, gas fireplace, iron, A/C, TV, hair dryer, 2 phone lines, voice mail and data ports with high-speed Internet access.

EXPENSIVE

Cascade Lodge ✱   You can't miss the Whistler Cascade Lodge, conveniently located on the left-hand corner as you drive down Village Gate Boulevard. This newish property (opened in 1998) in Village North is a 10-minute walk to the Whistler Base lifts, and the local bus stops across the street. Everything at the Cascade Lodge is built for efficiency, with a cursory nod to mountain-styling, such as the fireplace in the smallish lobby when you enter. It's a good spot for families, with fully stocked kitchens in the one- and two-bedroom suites, close to grocery shopping at the Whistler Marketplace, and an easy walk to restaurants. An in-suite laundry helps as well. The beds are comfortable; the soaker tubs are deep. The lodge boasts the largest outdoor pool in Whistler, plus two hot tubs. The pool deck is heated in winter. There's also a well-equipped gym for keeping fit, and dry saunas on the main floor. This is a self-service lodge, so be prepared to wash your towels if you want them fresh daily. The Resort Xtras Program is available (see Le Chamois for details).

4315 Northlands Blvd., Whistler, BC V0N 1B4. © **800/777-0185** or 604/905-4875. Fax 604/905-4089. www.whistler-cascadelodge.com or www.whistlerlodgingco.com. 152 units. Winter: C$260 (US$162.50) 1 bedroom, C$400 (US$250) 2 bedrooms. Summer: C$230 (US$143.75) 1 bedroom, C$320 (US$200) 2 bedrooms. Parking C$10 (US$6.25) per night in winter, C$8 (US$5) per night in summer. AE, MC, V. **Amenities:** Wheelchair accessible. Bike/ski storage (guests supply locks), outdoor pool, 2 hot tubs, fitness room, men's and women's saunas, 24-hour front desk, common laundry facilities. *In room:* Studio suites have kitchenettes, all others have a fully equipped kitchen, washer/dryers in 1- and 2-bedroom suites and some studios, iron, A/C, TV, hair dryer.

Legends Whistler Creek ✱✱   New and out-of-the-Village are two advantages of the Legends lodge at the base of the Creekside Gondola for ski-in/ski-out ease. New is a plus because you get to stay in a lodge that opened in mid-March 2001. Out-of-the-Village is a plus because the rates are lower to attract customers. Units are owned by quarter-share buyers, with a certain number rented out as hotel suites. An Intrawest development, Legends will soon be joined by luxury properties built along the same lines, and thus will the face of

Whistler Resort Accommodations

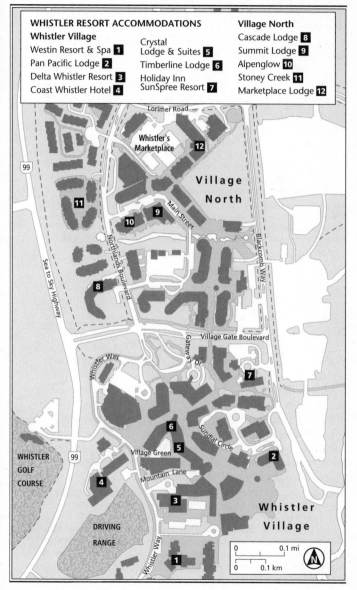

WHISTLER RESORT ACCOMMODATIONS

Whistler Village

Westin Resort & Spa **1**
Pan Pacific Lodge **2**
Delta Whistler Resort **3**
Coast Whistler Hotel **4**

Crystal Lodge & Suites **5**
Timberline Lodge **6**
Holiday Inn SunSpree Resort **7**

Village North

Cascade Lodge **8**
Summit Lodge **9**
Alpenglow **10**
Stoney Creek **11**
Marketplace Lodge **12**

lowly Creekside change forever. The one- to three-bedroom condo-style suites come with living room, dining area, and full-kitchen facility. Even one-bedrooms have two TVs. Two- and three-bedroom suites have 1.5 bathrooms and a variety of floor plans. Some have vaulted ceilings, a nice touch. Your family will enjoy the large pool and family hot tub, pool table, fitness room, outdoor BBQ to cook your own food, children's playroom, and movie room showing two movies a night. Whistler Mountain and the Creekside Gondola are right outside the door.

2036 London Lane, Whistler, BC V0N 1B2. © **800/332-3152.** Fax 604/689-9534. www.lodgingovations.com. 77 units. Winter C$149–C$358 (US$93.10–US$223.75) 1 bedroom, C$199–C$539 (US$124.35–US$336.85) 2 bedrooms. Summer C$99–C$212 (US$61.85–US$132.50) 1 bedroom, C$149–C$284 (US$93–US$177.50) 2 bed-rooms. Parking C$15 (US$9.35) per night. AE, MC, V. **Amenities:** Wheelchair acces-sible. 24-hour concierge, lounge area with gas fireplace, free hot apple cider in the lobby, ski and bike lockers, 2 pools, 2 Jacuzzis, fitness center, children's game room, movie room, concierge. *In room:* Full kitchen, gas fireplace, home entertainment center, direct modem line, soaker tub, private balcony, washer/dryer, hair dryer.

Lost Lake Lodge 🐸🐸🐸   You'll love this quiet forest setting over-looking the second hole of Chateau Whistler Golf Course. Ask for a room facing the course; otherwise you face the road but are never-theless fairly set back. The quality is exceptional, with Kohler fixtures in the bathroom, a full kitchen, fireplace, two televisions, and in-suite washer/dryers. The queen or king beds are among the best in Whistler, sizable with silky soft bedding. When you're in your studio, or one- or two-bedroom suite, it quickly feels like a very comfortable, good-quality home. While it's located on the Blackcomb Benchlands above the Upper Village, and fairly far from the Village (a 15-min. walk), a free bus shuttle runs frequently with a stop right outside the lodge. Lost Lake Park, with access to the Whistler Valley Trail, is right next door for strolling, biking, or cross-country skiing. Partial housekeeping service (unless you ask for full) includes daily garbage removal and fresh towels. Resort Xtras Program is available (see Le Chamois for details).

6440 Blackcomb Way, Whistler, BC V0N 1B4. © **800/777-0185** or 604/905-7631. Fax 604/905-0365. www.whistler-lostlakelodge.com. 99 units. Winter: C$259 (US$161.85) 1 bedroom, C$389 (US$243.10) 2 bedrooms. Summer: C$210 (US$131.25) 1 bedroom, C$295 (US$184.35) 2 bedrooms. Parking C$8–C$12 (US$5–US$7.50). AE, DC, DISC, MC, V. **Amenities:** 4 wheelchair accessible units. Ski/bike storage, pool, hot tub, exercise room, games room with billiards table, Internet station in lobby, 24-hour front desk. *In room:* TV/VCR, washer/dryer, hair dryer, efficiency or full kitchen.

A Ceiling Painted with Real Gold

Some things are worth noting: The gold-leaf domed ceiling at the Fairmont Chateau Whistler. The special lift at Westin Resort & Spa to carry a guest in a wheelchair plus attendant down to the Spa Club area. The Summit Lodge's pool and hot tub nestled amongst the evergreens in Village North. The view of Green Lake from The Edgewater Lodge. True ski in/ski out at the Residence Inn by Marriott. The super-comfy bed at Lost Lake Lodge. The convivial spirit of Alpine Lodge Pension. The brand-new log cabins at Riverside RV Resort & Campground. The very helpful staff at Crystal Lodge and the coupon package I received on arrival. A feeling "just like home" at Northstar at Stoney Creek.

Some things I wish were different: Drunks in the hot tubs. Uncomfortable beds that should be replaced by owners. Young men yelling after a night at a club. Marketers (of time shares, club memberships, and so on) who won't give you a straight answer. Stuffy lofts. Pools shut down for maintenance.

Summit Lodge ✦✦✦   Regarded as the premier boutique hotel in Whistler, Summit Lodge well deserves the accolades. Candles glow amidst the smooth, wet rocks in the floor-to-ceiling stone fountain, and tranquility-inducing aromas waft through the air. Wood and stone wrap around the lobby of the intimate lodge, which is located in Village North. This Kimpton Group property features one-bedroom suites and executive and deluxe studios, all with fully equipped kitchenettes and gas fireplaces. Luxurious down duvets and pillows on the very comfortable beds and pull-out couches give the Summit a high snuggle factor. Book a room in the back, where it's especially quiet. Overlooking the pool and hot tub, sip coffee on the heated balcony and look for Whisky Jacks, a local bird, in the evergreen trees. The hotel is generous with towels, kimonos, and made-in-BC Escents toiletries. The super-clean rooms are comfortable for families but intimate enough for romantic getaways. Kids' games at the front desk, as well as in-house babysitting available. Step out the door for restaurants, pharmacy, and grocery store. There's a personal grocery shopper if you want to cocoon.

4359 Main St., Whistler, BC V0N 1B4. ℂ **888/913-8811**, 604/932-2778. Fax 604/932-2716. www.summitlodge.com. 81 units. Winter: C$235 (US$146.85) 1 bedroom; C$165 (US$103) executive studio. Summer rates: C$229 (US$143) 1 bedroom; C$159 (US$99.35) executive studio. Parking C$15 (US$9.35) winter; C$10 (US$6.25) summer. AE, DC, DISC, MC, V. **Amenities:** Wheelchair accessible, concierge, free ski shuttle to Village and gondolas, ski technician on-site. Ski/bike/luggage storage, coin-operated laundry, room service breakfast available, 24-hr. front desk, pool, hot tub, exercise room. *In room:* A/C, TV/VCR, minibar, hair dryer.

Timberline Lodge   This cozy lodge on the Village Stroll is right in the heart of Whistler Village, 2 minutes from the gondolas and across from the Whistler Conference Centre. The location and fairly decent price attract a younger set, who enjoy being close to nightlife, restaurants, shops, and the Whistler Golf Course driving range. Built in 1987 and renovated in 1995, it's an older accommodation with European-style rustic features through the lobby and guest rooms. Large wooden frame beds and fireplaces are featured in most units (some studios excluded). The rooms are quite spacious, many with lofts and dens. Rooms range from studios with a Murphy bed (maximum occupancy four) to one-bedroom with loft (maximum six). All suites have a kitchenette or fully equipped kitchen. Everything is convenient from this location, including pharmacy, grocery stores, cafes, and clubs. The Resort Xtras Program is available (see Le Chamois for details).

4122 Village Green, Whistler, BC V0N 1B4. ℂ **800/777-0185** or 604/932-5211. Fax 604/932-2306. www.whistler-timberline.com or www.whistlerlodgeco.com. 44 units. Winter: C$259 (US$161.85) 1 bedroom, C$289 (US$180.60) 1 bedroom and loft. Summer: C$200 (US$125) 1 bedroom, C$240 (US$150) 1 bedroom and loft. Parking C$8 (US$5) per night in winter, C$12 (US$7.50) per night in summer. AE, DC, MC, V. **Amenities:** Wheelchair-accessible rooms, ski/bike storage, common laundry area, large pool, hot tub, sauna, common laundry facilities. *In room:* Some A/C units, TV/VCR, hair dryer.

Woodrun Lodge 𝄞𝄞   Get out of the Village and go slopeside on the Blackcomb Benchlands. This is a nice-looking property, with solicitous staff. The full facility lodge offers in-house front desk check-in, a concierge, and activity services. Enjoy free coffee served daily in the lobby, plus a free daily newspaper. In winter, it's ski in/ski out; in summer, it's close to the mountain for hiking and sightseeing. You can really pamper your family in these luxurious and spacious one- to three-bedroom suites (some with added dens). All have full kitchens, two bathrooms, fireplace, balconies, and in-suite laundry. Some of the suites have vaulted ceilings. The largest suite, at 160 sq. m (1,725 sq. ft.), is three-bedrooms/three-baths with a gigantic private

Jacuzzi in the master bedroom, two fireplaces, and a private view overlooking the mountain slope. In addition to the outdoor pool, it has the largest hot tub in Whistler. Being a 10-minute walk to the Village adds to the feeling of exclusivity.

4910 Spearhead Place, Whistler, BC V0N 1B4. © **888/267-6666**. Front desk © **604/ 932-6707**. Fax 604/932-6781. www.resortquestwhistler.com. 85 units. Winter: C$115–C$309 (US$71.85–US$193) 1 bedroom, C$130–C$409 (US$81.25–US$255.60) 2 bedrooms. Summer: C$92–C$260 (US$57.50–US$162.50) 1 bedroom, C$104– C$310 (US$65–US$193.75) 2 bedrooms. Parking C$10 (US$6.25) per night in winter, C$8 (US$5) per night in summer. AE, MC, DC, DISC, V. **Amenities:** Ski/bike storage (guests supply locks), fully equipped kitchens, small pool, large hot tub, exercise room. *In room:* Washer/dryers, iron, TV/VCR, hair dryer.

MODERATE

The Alpenglow   One of a number of newer accommodations, the lodge-style Alpenglow is in a great central location, with studio and one- and two-bedroom suites. Rooms are smaller than some, but are good value given the location, the price, and the big windows with lots of natural light. Some rooms face Main Street; preferred rooms face the mountains. All suites have fireplaces, fully equipped kitchens, and air-conditioning, which you don't find everywhere in the resort. The one-bedrooms have an additional pull-out couch or Murphy bed. Some units have deep, jetted tubs. The European-style luxury hotel has an enhanced, fully equipped fitness room, with lap pool, hot tub, steam room, and sauna. The Alpenglow tends to attract a younger, hipper crowd who view their accommodations as a base, not an end in itself. Within walking distance (maximum 10 min.) to lifts and 5 minutes to the Whistler Conference Centre, it's also in convenient Village North, with grocery store, post office, cafes, shops, and restaurants surrounding it. The bus stops nearby. Summit Service is available to all guests. Resort Xtras Program is available (see Le Chamois for details).

4369 Main St., Whistler, BC V0N 1B4. © **800/777-0185** or **604/932-2882**. Front desk 604/905-7078. Fax 604/905-7053. www.whistlerlodgingco.com. 87 units. Winter: C$239 (US$149.35) 1 bedroom, C$299 (US$186.85) 2 bedrooms. Summer: C$149–C$180 (US$93–US$112.50) 1 bedroom, C$250 (US$156.25) 2 bedrooms. Parking C$10 (US$6.25) per night in winter, C$8 (US$5) per night in summer. AE, DC, MC, V. **Amenities:** Wheelchair-accessible rooms available. Bike/ski storage with video surveillance (guests supply locks), common laundry facilities, pool, hot tub, fitness room, steam room, sauna, 24-hr. front desk. *In room:* A/C, iron, TV/VCR, hair dryer.

Coast Whistler Hotel   The price is right at the Coast, and if the room presented a bit of a squeeze getting the mini-fridge door open,

Whistler Valley Accommodations

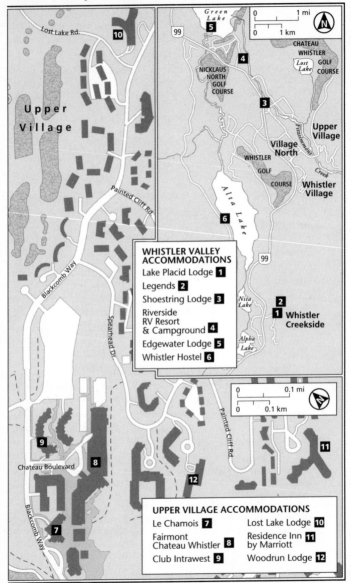

WHISTLER VALLEY ACCOMMODATIONS

Lake Placid Lodge **1**

Legends **2**

Shoestring Lodge **3**

Riverside RV Resort & Campground **4**

Edgewater Lodge **5**

Whistler Hostel **6**

UPPER VILLAGE ACCOMMODATIONS

Le Chamois **7**

Fairmont Chateau Whistler **8**

Club Intrawest **9**

Lost Lake Lodge **10**

Residence Inn by Marriott **11**

Woodrun Lodge **12**

that was all right too. Even though you're just across the road from the main Village, it's quiet here, especially if you ask for a room facing the Whistler Golf Course driving range. Our room smacked of Versailles with 11-foot-high windows swagged with drapes so as not to impede the great view of Whistler Mountain. A continental buffet-style breakfast comes with the room, with excellent coffee, muffins, croissants, cold cereal, fruits, and juice. The hotel was fully remodeled in 1997, and considering its location, it offers value for the money. Cross the road and you'll be paying twice as much. On-site services include an ATM and shiatsu and massage.

4005 Whistler Way. ℂ **800/663-5644.** Front desk 604/932-2522. Fax 604/932-6711. www.coastwhistlerhotels.com. 194 units. Winter: C$169 (US$105.60) standard hotel, C$189 (US$118) hotel superior, C$549 (US$343) 2 bedrooms. Summer: C$85 (US$53) standard hotel, C$95 (US$59.35) hotel superior, C$255 (US$159.35) 2 bedrooms. Parking $10 (US$6.25). AE, DC, MC, V. **Amenities:** Wheelchair rooms available, ski/bike storage, covered pool and hot tub, exercise room, sauna, concierge, ATM, daily housekeeping. *In room:* Mini-fridge, TV/VCR, hair dryer.

Crystal Lodge   One of the original lodgings in Whistler Village, the full-service Crystal Lodge has renovated its south wing with plans to do the north wing. Only a 2-minute walk to the gondolas, the combination of price and proximity is excellent. Staff are among the friendliest and most helpful of any I met, presenting me with a discount coupon package and brochures as well as a free paper daily. Staying here feels like you're staying with family and friends. A tuck shop and two popular family restaurants are on-site (Tex Corleone's and The Old Spaghetti Factory), plus the cozy, quiet Crystal Lounge. The Old Spaghetti Factory provides room service when you're too pooped after a day outdoors to get up and go out. Rooms are comfy, with standard king bed that can be split into twins. Units up to three bedrooms are available. If you want to get a good night's sleep, however, ask for the side away from the Village Stroll or bring earplugs. Revelers pass by in waves from the local clubs starting around midnight, and continue until 3am.

4154 Village Green, Whistler, BC V0N 1B4. ℂ **800/667-3363** or 604/932-2221. Fax 604/932-2635. www.crystal-lodge.com. 137 units. Winter: C$115 (US$71.85) hotel, C$135 (US$84.35) hotel deluxe, C$290 (US$181.25) 2 bedrooms. Summer: C$99 (US$61.85) hotel, C$119 (US$74.35) hotel deluxe, C$230 (US$143.75) 2 bedrooms. Parking C$8 (US$5) per night. AE, DC, DISC, MC, V. **Amenities:** Wheelchair accessible. Ski/bike storage, golf packages, lounge, restaurant, concession, heated outdoor pool and hot tub, indoor hot tub, sauna, outdoor pool, underground parking, guest laundry, dry cleaning. *In room:* Personal toiletries, A/C, TV, on-demand movies, Nintendo, mini-fridge, hair dryer.

Edgewater Lodge ⭐   A 12-unit lakeside retreat on 45 acres of beautiful, private, forested land, 3km (1.8 miles) north of Whistler Village overlooking Green Lake. The best part is the view through the picture windows, winter or summer, of mountains and lake. Because you're away from the resort proper, you can clearly see the stars at night. In summer, sit outside and watch a glorious sunset over the lake. Combine this with a gourmet restaurant on-site (see "Resort Dining" in chapter 4, "Where to Dine"), free parking, and a free gourmet continental breakfast, and this is one of the most unique places to stay in Whistler. Canoe from your doorstep or take a sleigh ride with Whistler Outdoor Experience (you'll pass it as you drive in). Golf at nearby Nicklaus North Golf Course. Six one-bedroom units include bathtub and extra pull-out twin bed. Six one-bedroom/den units come with a shower only. They include a king bed (which can be made into two twins), a pull-out twin, and a pull-out queen, making them a good choice for families. There are no coffeemakers in the rooms, but complimentary coffee and tea is offered in the dining room throughout the day.

8841 Hwy. 99. Mailing: Edgewater Lodge, Box 369, Whistler, BC V0N 1B0. Drive north of the Village on Hwy. 99 to the Alpine Way lights, turn right, then take the immediate first right down the short country lane to the end. © **604/932-0688.** Fax 604/932-0686. www.edgewater-lodge.com. 12 units. Winter: C$175–C$285 (US$109.35–US$178) 1 bedroom, C$215–C$320 (US$134.35–US$200) 1 bedroom/den. Summer: C$115–175 (US$71.85–US$109.35) 1 bedroom, C$145–C$215 (US$90.60–US$134.35) 1 bedroom/den. Midweek rates (all nights except Fri/Sat) are lower except for Dec 25–Jan 2. Children under 18 stay free. Free parking. AE, MC, V. **Amenities:** Bike/ski storage, hot tub, no pool, restaurant on-site, free continental breakfast, outdoor activity center, dogs stay for minimum C$20 (US$12.50) per night. *In room:* TV, VCR available, hair dryer.

Holiday Inn SunSpree   Steps away from Whistler and Blackcomb gondolas, the Holiday Inn is located in Whistler Village with great views of the mountains on all sides. It lacks a pool and you have to walk outdoors from the lobby to the elevator to your room. But convenience is everything. The inn has its own Activity Desk, where you can book lift tickets, sports, dining, and entertainment. In-room ski storage area is roomy, and a ski and snowboard lockup is also available at the front desk. After you check out, store your luggage with the front desk, leave your car in the underground parking, ski all day, then come back and freshen up in the fitness facility before you leave. The majority of rooms (95 of 115) are studios with bedding for two to four people. Additional adults C$25 (US$15.60) per night. One and two bedrooms also available. Every room includes a well-appointed kitchen and fireplace. Most have Jacuzzi-jetted tubs. As a safety feature, your room pass is needed to access your floor. Children 12 and under eat free at one of two nearby restaurants. Budget Rent-a-Car is located in the main lobby, and cars are available at the hotel.

4295 Blackcomb Way, Whistler, BC V0N 1B4. ℂ **800/229-3188,** 604/938-0878. Fax 604/938-9943. www.whistlerhi.com. 115 units, 6 allow smoking. Winter: C$139 (US$86.85) studio, C$169 (US$105.60) 1 bedroom. Summer: C$116 (US$72.50) studio, C$189 (US$118.10) 1 bedroom. Children 19 and under stay free. Parking C$11 (US$6.85) per night. AE, DC, DISC, MC, V. **Amenities:** Wheelchair accessible. Bike/ski storage, fitness facility, Jacuzzi, board games, videos for children, concierge, activity booking center, laundry. *In room:* Kitchen, TV, high-speed Internet access for a fee via TV, in-room movies, hair dryer. No A/C.

Lake Placid Lodge   Anyone looking for a good deal on accommodations looks to the Lake Placid Lodge. It's been around forever, an old standby at a good price. There's nothing fancy about it but it gets the job done, offering ski-in/ski-out access to the Creekside Gondola. In the summer, the inner courtyard with large pool and patio area is a real plus for family stays. The one- to three-bedroom suites come with gas fireplaces, private balconies with mountain or poolside views, and fully equipped kitchens. Some suites have new furnishings and carpet, and two bathrooms. For a quieter suite, ask for one overlooking the pool.

2050 Lake Placid Rd., Whistler, BC V0N 1B2. ℂ **800/663-7711.** Front desk 604/932-6699. Fax 604/932-2266. www.resortquestwhistler.com. 51 units. Winter: C$140–C$200 (US$87.50–US$125) 1 bedroom, C$235–C$300 (US$146.85–US$187.50) 2 bedrooms. Summer: C$110 (US$68.75) 1 bedroom, C$195 (US$121.87) 2 bedrooms. Children under 12 stay free. Free underground parking. AE, MC, V. **Amenities:** Wheelchair accessible. Bike/ski storage, full kitchen, big pool, hot tub, sauna, no fitness center, outdoor BBQs for use by guests, Creekside Kids Camp, common laundry. *In room:* TV/VCR, hair dryer. No A/C.

Northstar at Stoney Creek ⊛   The one- and two-bedroom suites have their own entrance, and feel just like home. The two-bedroom on two levels is ideal for families, with space to sleep up to six people. Two bathrooms (one full, one with shower), in-suite laundry (bring your own soap), full kitchen with ample room for cooking, television, and VCR all add up to a very comfortable stay. Flip on the gas fireplace and warm up while you watch TV or cook a meal. The pool area is quite large, with hot tub and heated deck (very nice for your feet on a wintry day). Changing rooms are spacious, and include saunas. Stoney Creek is located across the street from Whistler Marketplace in Village North, close to shopping and dining as well as the local bus system. My only complaint was that the beds in the owner-furnished rental suite where I stayed were the boxy kind you find in inferior hotels, with a lumpy foam placed over them in an attempt to make them more comfortable. It didn't work. If your suite has a basic flaw such as this, complain to the management. Overall, though, the location and setup of this complex (one of three by Northstar) made for an enjoyable and convenient extended stay.

4355 Northlands Blvd, Whistler, BC V0N 1B0. © 800/663-7711. Front desk 604/938-9666. Fax 604/905-3490. www.resortquestwhistler.com. 138 units. Winter: C$115–C$195 (US$71.85–US$121.85) 1 bedroom, C$130–C$280 (US$81.25–US$175) 2 bedrooms. Summer: C$125–C$189 (US$78–US$118) 1 bedroom, C$128–C$229 (US$80–US$143) 2 bedrooms. Free parking. AE, MC, V. **Amenities:** Large full kitchen, living area with gas fireplace, heated outdoor pool, common hot tub. *In room:* TV/VCR, washer/dryer, CD player, hair dryer.

Whistler's Marketplace Lodge   One look at the suites and you know this is where avid skiers and boarders stay. It's basic, it's minimal, and it's a relatively inexpensive place to enjoy the mountains. All suites feature a full kitchen, and a living and dining area with gas fireplace. Some suites offer a washer and dryer. What you give up is a pool, settling for an outdoor hot tub. Located right in Village North's Whistler Marketplace shopping complex, the lodge is close to everything you'd need for après-ski drinks, a quick nosh before crashing for the night, or a more elegant dining experience. In summer, you have easy access to golf clubs, tennis, activity centers for a number of activity providers, and a resort bus stop just across the way.

4360 Lorimer Rd., V0N 1B4. © 888/830-7031. Front desk 604/938-6699. Fax 604/932-6622. www.resortquestwhistler.com. 93 units. Winter: C$105 (US$65.62) hotel, C$140 (US$87.50) 1 bedroom, C$160 (US$100) 1 bedroom/den. Summer: C$79 (US$49.35) hotel, C$110 (US$68.75) 1 bedroom, C$125 (US$78) 1 bedroom/den. Free underground parking. AE, MC, V. **Amenities:** Ski/bike storage, hot tub, common laundry facilities. *In room:* Kitchenette or fully equipped kitchen, A/C in some units, TV/VCR, hair dryer.

2 Bed & Breakfasts

More than 25 B&B members are listed with the **Whistler Chamber of Commerce.** Contact them for a list (P.O. Box 181, Whistler, BC V0N 1B0, © 604/932-5528, fax 604/932-3755). A handful of B&Bs can be booked through **Whistler Central Reservations,** and the rest by calling direct. You can also contact the **Western Canada Bed and Breakfast Innkeepers Association** (© 604/255-9199, www.wcbbia.com), representing 100 inspected properties in Western

Canada. The **B.C. Bed and Breakfast Association** (© **605/734-3486,** www.bcbba.com) is an association of B&B reservation services and can also help.

Alpine Lodge Pension　No ordinary B&B, the Alpine Lodge is a cross between a European ski chalet and an upscale dorm. Rusty, the large ginger cat, greets guests in the stone-floored lobby. Travelers return for the great food and very relaxed atmosphere. An in-house chef, down duvets, the best steam room in Whistler, and gracious owner Geoffrey Carr make your stay memorable. Privacy is available in the detached "Dean Martin" suite with bath and kitchen that sleeps four and is perfect for families. The six-room Annex, with triple bunks and shared bath, is the place to book a family reunion or group travel. In the main building, rebuilt after a 1997 fire, all rooms have showers and views. Start the day with the complimentary, first-rate selection of breakfast items, served on the solid plank table. Book at least one of the optional dinners, deliciously prepared in the open kitchen while you relax in the vaulted-ceiling lounge. Guests can also cook in the fully equipped communal kitchen. The Alpine is a pension, so bring your own toiletries and facecloths. Towels are supplied.

8135 Alpine Way, Whistler, BC V0N 1B8. © **604/932-5966.** Fax 604/932-1104. www.alpinelodge.com. Drive north of Whistler Village, turning left at Alpine Way. Look for the lodge sign on the right. 8 units. Winter: C$120–C$275 (US$75–US$171.85). Summer: C$110–C$140 (US$68.75–US$87.50). Children under 12 stay free. Free parking. **Amenities:** In-house chef creates West Coast cuisine nightly, kitchen, indoor steam bath, indoor/outdoor Jacuzzis, 3 fireplaces, 2 large living areas, coin-operated laundry. Free shuttle bus, as well as available mountain guiding. *In room:* Most bedrooms have private baths, hair dryer.

Alpine Springs Bed and Breakfast　Owner James Sweeney opened his new B&B in February 2001, after 9 years with Four Seasons hotels. The house is only 5 years old, light, airy, with a modern feel. No knickknacks here. The main feature is the 65 sq. m (700 sq. ft.) sitting room/living room/dining area entirely for guest use. There's space to socialize, sit by the fireplace, watch TV from one set of sofas, or read a book at another. The three-level house is a comfortable, relaxed setting for individuals or a family visit. Next door is Meadow Park, with outdoor municipal barbecues for free use in the summer. Meadow Park Sports Centre is a 5-minute walk.

8314 Rainbow Dr., Whistler, BC V0N 1B8. © **888/833-3355** or 604-905-2747. Fax 604/905-2747. www.whistleralpinesprings.com. On Hwy. 99, drive past Whistler Village and Meadow Park Sports Centre, then turn left at Alpine Way traffic lights. At the 3-way intersection, turn left at Alpine Dr. onto Rainbow Dr., pass over speed bump, continue through a 4-way intersection to the 7th house on the left. 5 units. 1 suite, 2 rooms with queen, 2 rooms with twin bed. Winter: C$140–C$225 (US$87.50–US$140.60). Summer C$100–C$150 (US$62.50–US$93.75). Children 16 and under free. Full breakfast with hot entree included. V. Free parking. **Amenities:** Ski/bike storage, hot tub. Large sitting room with TV/VCR. *In room:* hair dryer.

Cedar Springs Bed & Breakfast Lodge   Guests at this charming, modern two-storey cedar and pine lodge have a choice of king-, queen-, or twin-size beds in modern yet understated surroundings. The sit-down gourmet breakfast (which includes a daily hot entree, homemade grain and fruit breads, and homemade preserves) is served by the wood-burning fireplace in the dining room. Guests are welcome to enjoy an afternoon tea with home-baked snacks. Owners Joern and Jacqueline Rohde can provide box lunches and special-occasion dinners at this cozy hideaway. The honeymoon suite has a wood-burning fireplace, private balcony, and CD/stereo. The guest sitting room has TV, VCR, video library, and complimentary tea and coffee. Inside there's a sauna; outside a hot tub on the sundeck overlooking the gardens. Adjacent to Meadow Park and the Valley Trail for biking, in-line skating, and walking, and a short walk to the Meadow Park Sports Centre. Complimentary shuttle in winter to the ski lifts, with public transit 2 minutes away.

8106 Cedar Springs Rd., Whistler, BC VON 1B8. ⓒ **800/727-7547** or 604/938-8007. Fax 604/938-8023. www.whistlerbb.com. 8 units, 6 with bathroom. Winter: C$109–C$279 (US$68–US$174.35) double. Summer: C$89–C$159 (US$55.60–$US99.35). Rates include full breakfast, tea, shuttle. Free parking. Complimentary pickup and drop-off from bus or train. AE, MC, V. Take Hwy. 99 north toward Pemberton 4km (2.4 miles) past Whistler Village. Turn left onto Alpine Way, go a block to Rainbow Dr. and turn left, go a block to Camino St. and turn left. The lodge is a block down, at the corner of Camino and Cedar Springs Rd. **Amenities:** Handicapped access on ground floor. Ski/bike storage, bike rentals available. *In room:* Hair dryer/iron available. Family room has double soaker tub, other rooms have shower only.

Durlacher Hof Pension Inn 𝒜𝒜   This traditional Alpine country inn boasts both superbly appointed guest rooms and a sociable atmosphere. Owners Peter and Erika Durlacher will greet you by name, hand you cozy slippers, then tour you through the two-storey chalet-style property. You can't help being impressed by the decor, which includes hand-carved pine furniture, extra-long twin or queen beds covered with goose-down duvets, and private baths with Jacuzzi tubs or showers. The views from the private balconies are impressive, and no telephone or television will disturb your tranquility. Downstairs there's a lounge, with a *kachelofen,* an old-fashioned fireplace oven. Guests linger over the complimentary (and lavish) hot breakfast featuring *kaiserschmarren*, a true Austrian sweet pancake. Later in the day, enjoy the welcoming fireplace and complimentary après-ski appetizers baked fresh daily by Erika. Afternoon social hours take place around the piano bar lounge licensed to serve liquor. Dinners with local chefs are available on selected evenings. Add to this a whirlpool, sauna, and well-chosen little library, and it's easy to see why so many guests return year after year.

7055 Nesters Rd., Whistler, BC V0N 1B7. ℂ **877/932-1924** or 604/932-1924. Fax 604/938-1980. www.durlacherhof.com. 8 units. Winter: C$185–C$230 (US$115.60–US$143.75), C$265 (US$165.60) premier rooms. Summer: C$120–C$199 (US$80–US$133). The inn is not suitable for children. Includes full breakfast and afternoon tea. Free parking. A minimum of 2 nights required for weekend stays in winter season. MC, V. Take Hwy. 99 1km (.62 mile) north of Whistler Village to Nesters Rd., and turn left. The inn is immediately on the right. **Amenities:** Wheelchair-accessible unit available. Ski/bike storage, breakfast/afternoon snacks complimentary, packed lunches can be arranged, sauna, whirlpool, heated bootroom, bus stop to lifts at doorstep. *In room:* Down duvets, fluffy bathrobes, slippers, hair dryer, no TV or telephone.

3 Real Deals

For additional low-cost accommodation listings, contact the **Whistler Chamber of Commerce** (P.O. Box 181, Whistler, BC V0N 1B0, ℂ **604/932-5528,** fax 604/932-3755).

Hostelling International Whistler   The location alone, not to mention the price, is worth the stay at the HI-Whistler Hostel. You find yourself far, far from the crowd on the west side of Alta Lake, in a former fishing lodge. Its reputation as one of the most beautiful hostels in Canada is well-deserved. Outdoor features include a deck and lawn looking over the lake to Whistler Mountain. Inside, the hostel is extremely civilized. Relax by the wood-burning stove, cook up your victuals in the common kitchen, eat in the dining room, play the piano or Ping-Pong. There's also a sauna, a drying room for ski gear, ski-waxing facilities, and storage for bikes, boards, and skis. In the summer, guests have use of a barbecue and canoes. There are eight dorm rooms, and one private room that can sleep up to four. Children must stay with family in the private room. Book by September at the latest for the winter ski season, and at least one week ahead in summer. Secured online reservations can be made at the website.

5678 Alta Lake Rd., Whistler, BC V0N 1B5. ℂ **604/932-5492.** Fax 604/932-4687. www.hihostels.ca. If driving from Vancouver on Hwy. 99, turn left at Alta Lake Rd.

before you reach Whistler Creekside. The hostel is on the right-hand side, 4.8km (3 miles) from the Hwy. 99 turnoff, and about 500m (1,640 ft.) past the speed bump. BC Rail (ⓒ 800/663-8238, www.bcrail.com) will drop you off at the hostel. Ask the conductor when boarding the train, since it's not a regular stop. From Whistler Village, take the Rainbow Park (4 buses daily in summer, 5 in winter). To walk, find the Valley Trail (behind the Royal Bank under the highway's underpass) and follow the trail 4km (2.4 miles) to Rainbow Park, then turn left on Alta Lake Rd. for another 400m (1,312 ft.). 31 beds in 4- to 6-bed dorms. C$19.50 (US$12) IYHA members, C$23.80 (US$14.85) non-members. Private room C$53.90 (US$33.70) members, C$62.45 (US$39) non-members (based on 2-person occupancy). Linen C$2 (US$1.25). Annual adult hostel membership C$37.45 (US$23.40). Family and group memberships available. MC, V. Free parking. **Amenities:** Bike/ski storage, common kitchen, sauna, BBQ, canoe. *In room:* Towels can be rented for 50¢.

Riverside RV Resort and Campground

This is one of the fanciest RV campgrounds I've come across, a 40-acre property beside the serene glacier-fed Fitzsimmons Creek. The big new lodge where you check in has an Internet cafe, grocery store, laundromat, games room, and activity center. The campground includes an 18-hole putting course and children's playground. But you don't have to come with RV or tent to stay—14 new log cabins are now available at Riverside. If you've never slept in a cozy log cabin, this is the place to start. The one-bedroom cabins are well soundproofed and quiet, and include a kitchenette. In addition to the private master bedroom with a queen bed, they have a hide-a-bed sofa in the living area and a loft where two can sleep on twin mattresses. Maximum number of adults per unit is four, or maximum of two adults with four children. Access to the loft is by a straight-up log ladder, and because you can't stand up in the loft, it's best for older children or youth. There's no bathtub in any of the units, only a shower. No smoking, no pets in cabins. Check-out time is 11am.

8018 Mons Rd., Whistler, BC V0N 1B0. ⓒ 877/905-5533. Fax 604/905-5539. www.whistlercamping.com. Drive 1.6km (1 mile) north of Whistler Village on Hwy. 99. Turn right on Blackcomb Way, then immediate left onto Mons Rd. Riverside is the next left. 14 log cabins. Winter: C$150–C$175 per night (US$93.75–US$109.35). Summer: C$125–C$150 per night (US$78–US$93.75). Children in a family unit stay free. Free parking. AE, MC, V. **Amenities:** Cabin 10 is fully wheelchair accessible. Internet cafe, grocery store, laundromat, games room, activity center, putting course, professionally designed sand volleyball court, children's playground. *In room:* Full kitchen, TV.

The Shoestring Lodge

Dark green doesn't show wear and tear, and there's lots of dark green at The Shoestring Lodge. The clientele is largely young, intent on skiing, boarding, mountain biking, and you-name-it sports activities. They hail from around the world, and want to stay in Whistler as long as they can, as cheaply as they can.

When you enter the dim lobby, the first thing you notice is the woodstove crackling by the beat-up couches, a welcoming touch. In addition to four-person and six-person dorm rooms with bunk beds and a TV, private double and queen rooms are available at a price far below the average Whistler rates. The rooms aren't fancy, but did you expect them to be? Add free parking and a free bus shuttle to the mountains in winter, and you can stay those extra days after all. Daily housekeeping service and en suite bathrooms.

7124 Nancy Greene Dr., Whistler, BC V0N 1B0. © **877/551-4954** or 604/932-3338. Fax 604/932-8347. www.shoestringlodge.com. North of Whistler Village off Hwy. 99. Turn left at Nancy Greene Dr. 22 private units, 24 shared dorm rooms. Winter C$28–C$32 (US$17.50–US$20) per person 4-share, queen/double rooms C$95–C$139 (US$59.35–US$86.85). Summer C$17–C$22 (US$10.60–US$13.75) per person 4-share, queen/double rooms C$60–C$80 (US$37.50–US$50). Free parking. AE, MC, V. **Amenities:** Ski/bike storage, pub, restaurant, beer and wine store, 24-hr. front desk, common laundry, volleyball court. *In room:* Bedding, towels, some private rooms and 2 dorm rooms have bathtubs, all others have showers, TV.

4

Where to Dine

For a place that started with lakeside fish fries, Whistler has transformed into a diner's paradise, a grazing ground that compares favorably with major international centers. More than 93 eating establishments range from fine French and West Coast cuisine to hole-in-the-wall cafes. You can literally take your pick of what to eat anywhere in the resort, with some gems tucked out of the way beyond the Village. Many of the restaurants have won awards, with two hotels, The Westin Resort & Spa and the Fairmont Chateau Whistler, rated in Condé Nast publications' top 20 list for resort food and lodgings worldwide.

Some of British Columbia's top chefs reside and work in Whistler, as well as some superb younger chefs making their way up at more moderately priced establishments. The restaurant scene is extremely competitive, and even cafes and coffee shops have to set high standards.

Serious dollars are spent here year-round, and visitors want quality for what they spend. The chefs are more than happy to please. Over the past decade, they have looked to the Pemberton Valley to the north, where organic market gardeners have emerged to satisfy their penchant for locally grown produce, fresh fruit, fish, and meat. Other BC produce comes from the Okanagan, famous for its fruit, and the Fraser Valley near Vancouver. Local and regional foods range from berries to mushrooms and smoked salmon to venison.

The array of wines and depth of their selection is another lure to diners at Whistler. Wines from British Columbia continue to grow in reputation, with top-quality BC red wines making their presence felt in the past 10 years, joining the already popular white varieties. California wines attract US visitors, who find they can enjoy them here for less than back home. Many discerning owners and executive chefs stock top international wines.

A 7% tax is added to your food bill, and a 17% tax to wines. A tip of 15% to 20% on the total bill is standard practice.

If going out isn't on your agenda but you'd like to try the food, you can order in from dozens of local restaurants with either Whistler Valet Services (© **604/905-6444,** 11am to 11pm daily) or Resort Room Service (© **604/905-4711,** summer 4pm to 11pm; winter 11am to 11pm). Their free brochures are easily found around the Resort. The Whistler telephone book has an extensive restaurant menu section to help you make your choices. And if the bulk of your money is spent on lift tickets, you can still eat out or order in from more than a dozen fast food and pizza places with free delivery.

Because so many visitors now stay in condo-style accommodations, many vary eating out with cooking at home. Four grocery stores, **The Grocery Store** (© **604/932-3628**) at 4211 Village Square in the Village, **IGA Plus** (© **604/932-3628**) at 4330 Northlands Blvd. in Whistler Marketplace, **Nesters Market** (© **604/932-3545**) outside the Village in Nesters Square mall, and **Food Plus** (© **604/ 932-6193**) at 107-2011 Innsbruck Dr. in Creekside, stock their shelves with produce that will satisfy any gourmet cook. They also sell dozens of brands of quick snacks like nachos and chips for the armies of young people who come to ski and snowboard.

For **après-ski dining,** see chapter 8, "Whistler After Dark."

1 Mountain Dining

WINTER SEASON

If your idea of the perfect place to eat includes mile-high views, both Whistler and Blackcomb mountains do the job well. During the ski season, a total of 15 on-mountain eating establishments are active. The main eating area on Whistler Mountain is Roundhouse Lodge, and on Blackcomb it's The Rendezvous. Both mountains have one higher-end dining area (Blackcomb's Christine's, and Whistler's Steeps Grill), as well as a selection of market-style (cafeteria-format) cafes, delis, and ski-in eateries.

You can dine on the mountains in summer, but there are restrictions at the present time. Whistler Mountain is closed from around June 10 to July 1 for lift maintenance. On the July 1 weekend (Canada's birthday), the Roundhouse opens its Mountain Market with an outdoor BBQ and patio. Live entertainment is sometimes included for a "mountain beach" atmosphere for visitors who come up to hike, sightsee, or just to tan.

Blackcomb Mountain is open for summer glacier skiing and race and mogul camps. Thus far, non-skiers have been out of luck. This may change as Blackcomb's chairs provide amazing access to the high alpine. Mountain management is considering opening the area to summer sightseeing. If so, The Rendezvous may be open to serve soups, sandwiches, and picnic-style food.

Whistler-Blackcomb's strategy is to offer unique dining experiences in the various on-mountain spots. Each dining area has a signature item to differentiate it from its cousins. Here's a rundown of what you'll find.

Tips **Time for Lunch!**

Beat the lunch-hour rush, and eat before 11:30am or after 1pm. Line-ups will be shorter. The Huts (The Chic Pea, Raven's Nest, Crystal Hut, or Horstman Hut) are all cozy, quick places to eat.

WHISTLER MOUNTAIN

One of the best winter deals on Whistler Mountain is called Fresh Tracks. Take the Whistler Village Gondola between 7:15am and 8:30am to watch the sun come up at the 4,645 sq. m (50,000 sq. ft.) **Roundhouse Lodge** with an all-you-can-eat breakfast buffet for C$16 (US$10). The bonus is that, once Whistler Mountain is cleared by avalanche control, you're free to carve up powder before regular skiers get there.

To refuel on your way to yet another run, Roundhouse has quick-service menus at **Pikas,** a family-style hamburger spot with pizza and kids' meals too. **Paloma's** serves pizza, pasta, and minestrone soup, all good skier's fare. On the second floor is **Mountain Market** with Asian bowls and salads.

To catch your breath over lunch with 360-degree views of the busy high alpine peaks, try **Steeps Grill** (© **604/932-3434**). Here is a real find at 1,158m (3,800 vertical ft.), a sit-down restaurant where skiers can catch up with their triumphs on the slopes. It was a big surprise to find one of the best meals in Whistler at the top of a gondola, and at an affordable price. For starters, order a glass of white or red wine at C$6.50 to C$7 (US$4.05 to US$4.35). The signature appetizer, chowder made with smoked and fresh Pacific salmon, is by itself worth the trip up. Follow with a pure BC experience, a grilled 226-gram (8-oz.) Coho salmon filet with seasonal vegetables and turmeric rice for C$14 (US$8.75). For meat eaters, the braised lamb shank in a rosemary Merlot jus, served with ratatouille vegetables and pumpkin mashed potatoes, will wow you at C$15 (US$9.35). In spring, the menu changes to lighter fare. Lunch is served from 11am to 2:30pm. If you're a non-skier, go to the ticket window at the Whistler Gondola base and buy a sightseer's pass, C$22 (US$13.75) for adults, C$14 (US$8.75) for children 7 to 12 years, and C$19 (US$11.85) for youths 13 to 18 and seniors 65 and over. The gondola is fully enclosed, and you exit a few steps from the Roundhouse.

Other spots on the mountain are designed for skiers and boarders, not sightseers. The Green Run provides easy access to **The Chic Pea,** a cabin with a huge, sunny patio, giant cinnamon buns, pizza, and hot subs. At the top of the Creekside Gondola you'll find **Raven's Nest,** a Whistler original with a valley-view deck and an outdoor grill. You can also get fresh sandwiches, chili, soups, baked goods, and cappuccino. **Harmony Hut,** at the top of Harmony Express Chair, is really a warming hut, a place to shelter from winds at 2,115m (6,939 ft.) and refuel with a hot stew or apple cider. It does have outstanding views of Black Tusk and the Coast Mountains, but you have to ski down from here. **Nestlé Kit-Kat Snack-Shack** is a ski-through kiosk for chocolate, drinks, and gourmet hot dogs (sometimes even BBQ) at the base of Harmony Express.

Fun Fact   **Award-winning Wines of BC**

Confronted with the huge selection of British Columbia wines in Whistler, what do you order? Start with award-winning wines produced in the dry climate of the southern Okanagan. Mission Hill Winery, located in Westbank in the Okanagan Valley, was named Winery of the Year by *Wine Access* magazine based on the consistency of its top-ranked wines. Tinhorn Creek 1998 Merlot, from 100% Merlot grape grown in "the golden mile" in the south Okanagan, took red wine of the year in the Canadian Wine Awards 2000. Mission Hill Estate 1999 Chardonnay won the Gold Medal in the Chardonnay du Monde Competition in St. Lager, France, in March 2001.

Whistler sommeliers and maître'd's are well-qualified to guide you through extensive collections from the Okanagan, as well as smaller BC wineries located in the Similkameen Valley, on Vancouver Island, and in the Fraser

Valley. Hawthorne Mountain Vineyards 2000 Chardonnay Gold Label Series from the Similkameen Valley won white wine of the year in the Canadian Wine Awards. Cherry Point, Blue Grouse, and Venturi Schulze are Vancouver Island boutique wineries. The Fraser Valley's Domaine de Chaberton and Township 7 produce small quantities of remarkable wine.

Icewine, made from grapes picked frozen, is now a British Columbia specialty. *Icewine, The Complete Story* by local wine expert John Schreiner relates the ingenuity of winemakers who awoke to find their vineyards frozen. Jackson-Triggs 2000 Riesling Icewine Proprietor's Reserve is a gold-medal winner.

BLACKCOMB MOUNTAIN

The Rendezvous, at 1,860m (6,102 ft.), is first for dining on Blackcomb Mountain. Take the Wizard Express, then the Solar Coaster Express. Eat your breakfast here or make it lunch with a real variety of choices, including Mexican-style fajitas and enchiladas, soup, salads, and BBQ. For something quite different, enjoy full-service dining at **Christine's** (© **604/938-7437**). With its white linen tablecloths and air of casual elegance, Christine's is a step up from Steeps Grill. The menu includes Pacific Northwest favorites, a good choice of wine, and a beautiful view westward into Whistler Valley. Try the stew with fish and shellfish from local waters, the warm spinach salad with goat cheese and caramelized bacon, and the chef's daily pasta feature, such as portobello mushroom–stuffed ravioli. Christine's is most easily accessed by skiers.

Glacier Creek Lodge at 1,545m (5,069 ft.) is another outstanding mountain eatery with two restaurants. The market-style Glacier Creek serves up Asian stir-frys; **BCeatery** features West Coast food such as a cream-style chowder with halibut and salmon.

Ski or board in, or take a Canadian Snowmobile snowmobile or Snowcat tour, to visit **Crystal Hut,** a snug Canadiana cabin serving home-style fare and its justifiably famous Canadian waffles. The hut is located at 1,844m (6,053 ft.) with a wood-burning oven roasting meats and fish. The view from the back deck scans the whole of Whistler Valley and the mountains beyond.

Horstman Hut, at 2,284m (7,494 ft), is the final frontier for steaming stews, chili, and macaroni and cheese. This is the gateway to the backcountry, accessible to more skilled athletes. Because of its unique location on the mountain, skiers stop here to warm up with high-calorie entrees. If you're a black diamond skier, the word is that on a sunny day the view from the outdoor BBQ area is spectacular. Facing the southerly Coast Mountains, you'll see Black Tusk, The Lions, and other peaks.

On your way back to base, ski through the **Nestlé Kit-Kat Snack-Shack** for hot drinks, chocolate, and hot dogs at the base of Excelerator Chair.

Value Wine & Dine Celebration

November is the month for Cornucopia, Whistler's food and wine celebration. If you love food, this is the place to be, with a reputation that is growing internationally. The haute cuisine extravaganza celebrates the cuisines and specialties of the Pacific West Coast. The 3-day event starts with a gala grand tasting of more than 50 top Pacific Coast wineries and gourmet grazing, for C$100 (US$62.50) in the Westin Resort & Spa. Winemakers' dinners, chefs' showcases, a celebrity chef cook-off, and food and wine seminars culminate with Sunday's farewell brunch featuring international fare and premier wines. Package deals including accommodation start at C$439 (US$299) and will save you money. If you're already staying in Whistler, the Event Tickets Only Package is available. Reserve early, since Cornucopia has really grown in popularity. And get out your fancy duds; this is worth dressing up for.

AT THE BASES

At the mountain bases you can ski right up to the deck of three restaurants. At Garibaldi Lift Co. in Whistler Village, you'll find a large restaurant pub with a heritage atmosphere, rated as one of North America's best après-ski bars by *Ski Magazine*. Dusty's Bar & BBQ in Creekside is a relaxing place for lunch, and rocks with nightly entertainment and an award-winning patio BBQ. Merlin's Bar & Grill at Blackcomb Base serves lunch and dinner late into the evening with the resort's largest outdoor patio.

For coffee, stop at Blackcomb Base's Wizard Grill for espresso, a pancake breakfast, or a bagel. At the Whistler Village Gondola base, Essentially Blackcomb has steaming lattes and an "Egg & Ride" special. At Creekside, Whistler's original base, visit Dusty's Backside for breakfast burritos, blueberry pancakes, muffins, snacks, and espresso.

2 Resort Dining

VERY EXPENSIVE

Araxi Restaurant & Bar WEST COAST   Araxi's owner Jack Evrensel named his restaurant after his wife. That was 20 years ago, and since then the renowned restaurateur couple continue to win awards for their menu and wine list. The decor is coolly sophisticated, with pale earth tones, leather banquets, and a giant Italian urn or two. But it's not the decor that draws people; it's the wines. Voted "Best Restaurant in Whistler" many times, Araxi was recently treated to an expensive overhaul to provide storage for a 12,000-bottle inventory of exceptional British Columbia and foreign wines. Wine director and sommelier Chris Van Nus is more than happy to suggest a suitable vintage. Under the direction of executive chef Scott Kidd, the menu is decidedly West Coast (with Italian and French influences), answering to the love of local produce. Start with an appetizer of smoked Salt Spring Island Albacore tuna, or Pemberton Pumpkin ravioli with toasted Aldergrove hazelnuts. Move on to British Columbia seafood risotto or peppered Barbary duck breast with leek and fig tart, organic quince preserve, and sweet and sour shiitake jus. For straightforward meat lovers, there's Alberta AAA Beef Tenderloin, among other meat dishes.

4222 Village Square, Whistler Village. ⓒ **604/932-4540**. Main courses C$24–C$38 (US$15–US$23.75). AE, DC, MC, V. Daily 5pm–11pm. Bar and lounge open to midnight.

The Aubergine Grille WEST COAST   The 150-seat indoor/ 80-seat outdoor restaurant is finished with unusual materials such as river rock, log ends, and hickory sticks. The view from the floor-to-ceiling windows is of Rainbow and Sproat mountains. But the focus of attention is on the show kitchen, where you watch chefs prepare breakfast, lunch, and dinner. Swiss-born executive chef Hans Stierli trained in his homeland before coming to Canada in 1987. He headed straight for the top, opening The Aubergine Grille in the new Westin Resort & Spa in Whistler in June 2000 with an exceptional wine list to boot. The menu includes West Coast seafood and salmon favorites, plus comfort food selections of grilled meats and rustic pizza and pasta entrees. Highly recommended is the absolute melt-in-your-mouth fire-grilled filet of certified Angus Beef with Café de Paris butter on roasted farmers' vegetables and garlic-roasted organic marble vegetables. Finish up with the chef's special dessert, such as a Study of Brulée, five ramikens of brulées from pistachio to mocha delivered with a flourish on a piece of slate. An unbelievable sugar rush follows. The FireRock Lounge (open from 11am to 1am) adjacent to the restaurant is an intimate spot for a quiet drink within the hotel confines.

4090 Whistler Way in the Westin Resort & Spa, Whistler Village. ✆ **604/935-4344.** Main courses C$20–C$45 (US$12.50–US$28.10-). AE, MC, V. Daily 7am–10pm.

Bear Foot Bistro FRENCH Hands down, this is the most expensive restaurant in Whistler with a C$85 (US$53.10) three-course table d'hote–style menu, a chef's five-course tasting menu for C$100 (US$62.50), and a chef's *menu gastronomique* for C$200 (US$125). Is it worth it? Let's just say that a brigade of 20 chefs serves the two-floor, 110-seat dining room, cooking up fresh game such as elk, buffalo, and the signature loin of wild Arctic caribou in a state-of-the-art open kitchen. In only 5 years, owner André Saint Jacques has won many honors for his wine list, with 14,000 bottles and 1,300 labels in his cellar. The champagne selection is second to none, and includes Dom Perignon and Veuve Cliquot by the glass. Add live jazz on winter weekends, the largest selection of Cuban cigars in any restaurant in BC, plus a secluded smoking room and valet parking. The Bear Foot Wine Bar is a hidden gem next door, with more casual French bistro seating for 50, serving more afford-able classic steak tartare, foie gras, and up to 20 wines available by the glass.

4121 Village Green in Listel Hotel, Whistler Village. ✆ **604/932-3433.** Reservations recommended. Main courses C$85–C$200 (US$53.10–US$125). Daily 6pm–10pm.

La Rua Restaurante WEST COAST With its smudged dark cherry-colored walls, pools of light, sensuous artwork, and warm ambiance, La Rua will make you feel utterly pampered and decidedly international. Voted *Vancouver* magazine's Gold Medal award-winner for 5 consecutive years, the restaurant's great food and great wines are the joint love of owner Mario Enero and executive chef R.D. Stewart. From the attentive staff to the exciting main courses, their commitment to please their customers is obvious from the moment you step in the door. Six pasta dishes join entrees such as

BC salmon with a fresh horseradish crust and lemon balm butter, or a cassoulet of lamb with Toulouse sausage, confit of duck, haricot, and navy beans. Check out the daily fresh sheet prepared by chef Stewart. This is where he tries new and creative dishes like agnolotti stuffed with duck confit and fresh morel mushrooms, or filet of ostrich roasted and served with stilton mash, scarlet plum, and cranberry jus. Depending on your response, the items on the fresh sheet may one day end up on the main menu. In the summer, you can watch the moon pop up over Blackcomb Mountain from the 80-seat patio.

4557 Blackcomb Way in Le Chamois, Upper Village. ℂ **604/932-5011.** Reservations highly recommended. Main courses C$18–C$36 (US$11.25–US$22.50). AE, DC, MC, V. Daily 6pm–10pm.

Quattro Ristorante ITALIAN A palate of rich mahogany, umbers, and ochers and hand-painted silk chandeliers contribute to a warm but not stuffy atmosphere at Quattro. The Venetian-style decor is a prelude to the flavors of country Italian cooking and a 900-label wine list. Radicchio Bocconcini, a grilled fresh mozzarella wrapped with prosciutto and radicchio in a cherry vinaigrette, is a tantalizing starter. Mop up the vinaigrette with the fresh-baked bread, and taste your partner's Polpette di Mare, a little Dungeness crab and sea scallop cake with moscato and chive aioli. For your main course, Fusilli Tartufati is a sensational experience combining hand-rolled fusilli, wild mushroom, sage, white truffle oil, and shaved parmigiano reggiano in a light cream. Galletto al Mattone is a panini grill-pressed with marinated, deboned cornish game hen that is best with generous squeezes of fresh lemon. If you still have room, the warm chocolate cake topped with a tiny crown of spun sugar is heavenly. A fireplace in winter and patio dining in summer makes Quattro a year-round favorite.

4319 Main St., behind Delta Pinnacle, Village North. ℂ **604/905-4844.** Reservations recommended. Main courses C$18.95–C$36.95 (US$11.85–US$23.10). AE, DC, MC, V. Daily 5:30pm–11pm. Closed first 2 weeks in Nov.

Rimrock Café SEAFOOD AND GAME Park in the free parking lot, then head upstairs to the big welcoming room filled with enthusiastic diners. It's the ambience that draws people to the Creekside location of the Rimrock Café. If you like seafood, the fish trio will jump out at you, combining pan-seared ahi tuna, sea bass, and grilled prawns with roasted tomato salsa. Or if you're in the mood for a combo, the surf and turf with a filet steak and Atlantic lobster will fill the bill. But don't forget to start with the cafe's favorite appetizer of a half dozen oysters, served one of six different ways by Chef Rolf Gunther. Try the Rasputin, a raw oyster prepared with crème fraîche and lumpfish caviar. The accompanying wine list has a number of fine vintages from BC, California, New Zealand, and Australia, also available by the glass. Rimrock placed first in the Whistler Zagot Survey, received a three-star vote in *Northwest Best Places,* and two stars in *Where to Eat in Canada.*

2117 Whistler Rd., Creekside. © **604/932-5565.** Reservations recommended. Main courses C$24–C$45 (US$15–US$28). AE, MC, V. Daily 6pm–9:30pm.

Val d'Isère FRENCH   Sitting on the patio at Val d'Isère watching the world go by makes you feel you are really, truly on holidays. Inside is just as delightful, with an appealing blue-and-gold Provençal decor that seems to float away on white linen. A summer children's menu is available while adults enjoy a taste of Alsace from owner and chef Roland Pfaff. In winter, begin with roast garlic soup with poached egg and croutons, or a more mellow Nova Scotia lobster bisque. Highlights of the menu include salmon and sea bass, pan-fried veal sweetbreads with Serrano Spanish ham, and roasted milk-fed veal with Vancouver Island morel mushroom sauce. Summer fare is in a lighter vein, such as the seared scallops with candied lemon/ginger sauce. Prices also drop in summer, making this restaurant a very good deal. Alsace wines feature highly on the impressive cellar list, but others from France, the US, and Canada are chosen by three certified sommeliers. For dessert (and you must have a dessert), choose any one of eight items, from a Study of Chocolate, an extravaganza of five chocolate confections for C$12.95 (US$8.10), to the delicate Ménage à Trois, a cornucopia of homemade sorbet.

4314 Main St., in Bear Lodge, Town Plaza, Village North. © **604/932-4666.** Reservations recommended. Main courses C$27–C$37 (US$16.85–US$23.10). AE, DC, MC, V. Daily 5pm–10pm.

The Wildflower WEST COAST   Every aspect of the Chateau is done up in a grand Canadiana style. You won't see anything less in The Wildflower, newly renovated to the tune of $1 million, now an imposing room in an expansive setting. Come hungry to the daily breakfast buffet, C$23 (US$14.35) or Sunday brunch, C$35 (US$21.85). Do try the sinfully good hot blueberry bread pudding. Lunch may be pasta or a sandwich on fresh-baked bread. The focus here is really on dinner, offering classic and regional entrees such as Fraser Valley duck, free range chicken and porcini mushroom pot au feu, and pepper-seared sterling silver rib-eye steak. The overall effect is that of West Coast/North American fare with an old-world,

Whistler Resort Dining

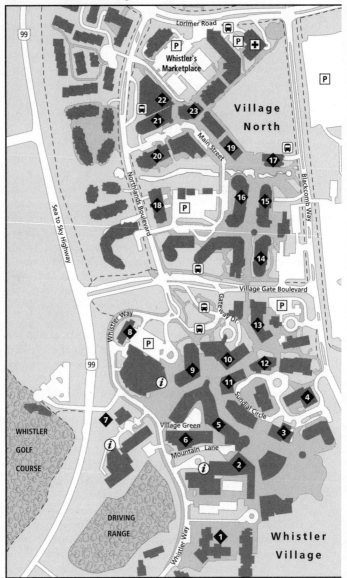

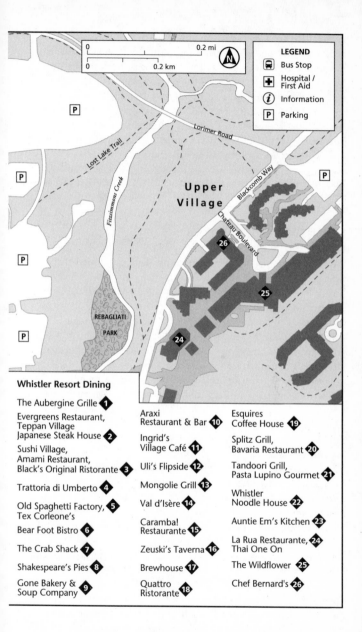

LEGEND

🚍 Bus Stop

✚ Hospital / First Aid

ⓘ Information

P Parking

Upper Village

REBAGLIATI PARK

Whistler Resort Dining

The Aubergine Grille ❶

Evergreens Restaurant,
Teppan Village
Japanese Steak House ❷

Sushi Village,
Amami Restaurant,
Black's Original Ristorante ❸

Trattoria di Umberto ❹

Old Spaghetti Factory,
Tex Corleone's ❺

Bear Foot Bistro ❻

The Crab Shack ❼

Shakespeare's Pies ❽

Gone Bakery &
Soup Company ❾

Araxi
Restaurant & Bar ❿

Ingrid's
Village Café ⓫

Uli's Flipside ⓬

Mongolie Grill ⓭

Val d'Isère ⓮

Caramba!
Restaurante ⓯

Zeuski's Taverna ⓰

Brewhouse ⓱

Quattro
Ristorante ⓲

Esquires
Coffee House ⓳

Splitz Grill,
Bavaria Restaurant ⓴

Tandoori Grill,
Pasta Lupino Gourmet ㉑

Whistler
Noodle House ㉒

Auntie Em's Kitchen ㉓

La Rua Restaurante, ㉔
Thai One On

The Wildflower ㉕

Chef Bernard's ㉖

French flair. The Chateau has an impressive collection of over 2,500 bottles of wine, chosen by manager and sommelier Fergus O'Halloran, recognized as one of Canada's top sommeliers. Stroll through the restaurant past the 6m-high (20-ft.) wine display cabinets to check out the private 18-seat wine-tasting room at the back. Executive chef Vincent Stefano oversees The Wildflower along with **The Mallard Bar** (© 604/938-8000), a lively après-ski and dinner lounge, and **Portobello** (© 604/938-2040), a casual upscale dining spot with open-style kitchen for breakfast, lunch, and dinner.

4599 Chateau Blvd., in The Fairmont Chateau Whistler, Upper Village. © **604/938-2033**. Reservations recommended. Main courses C$18–C$45 (US$12–US$28.10). AE, DC, DISC, MC, V. Daily 7am–11am, lunch 11am–2:30pm (high season only), dinner 6pm–10pm.

EXPENSIVE

Bavaria Restaurant EUROPEAN ALPINE CUISINE   This is the place where fellow chefs come to pay homage to food that is "special" and "unlike anywhere else." Owner Joel Thibault and his beautiful wife Angela create an indulgent atmosphere with the focus on traditional fondue and schnitzel. Start with Reiberdatschi Gorgonzola, a potato pancake with a voluptuous topping of gorgonzola cheese; or Joel's celebrated Raclette, melted cheese with potato and cold cuts, just right for kids or smaller appetites. Homemade bratwurst, tender sauerkraut, and freshly made *spaetzle* (a potato noodle) all tempt the palate, but save some room for the mains. Winter season features wild game dinners. Filet au Poivre, featuring Alberta beef, is smothered in brandy pepper sauce and is perfect for beef connoisseurs. The duck is from BC's Fraser Valley, succulent and rich. And the original Wiener schnitzel, a delicately breaded veal cutlet skillfully pan-fried, is an art form. Squeeze fresh lemon juice on top, and let your taste buds dance. Cheese or oil fondues are perfect for a group. House-made apple strudel and *Kaiserschmarrn,* a caramelized crepe with fresh fruit, elicit groans of appreciation. With Joel himself working the bar, singing and laughing with guests, this is the best place for comfort and fuel for the next day of skiing or hiking.

4369 Main St. at Alpenglow Hotel, Village North. © **604/932-7518**. Reservations recommended for peak season. Main courses C$22–C$32 (US$13.75–US$20). AE, MC, V. Daily 5:30pm–10pm (last order in before 10pm).

Creekside Grillroom BEEF, SEAFOOD   You'll feel like a local at the Creekside Grillroom with its mix of couples and families dining in a room that seats 50 max, with 30 additional patio seats in the summer. Much of the clientele is local, drawn by the homey atmosphere as well as the food and owner Ron Hozmer's extensive wine list. This place is loved and lived in, with a slightly frayed carpet that's refreshing after the excesses of the Village. The food definitely draws repeat visitors, including 10 variations of Alberta beef, from rib eye to grillroom filet. All steaks are Canadian AAA, aged a minimum of 28 days, so they really melt in your mouth. Or you might try the chicken and ribs, or the pan-seared ahi tuna and salmon, laid one on the other like an elegant pyramid over noodles and stir-fried vegetables laced with a fragrant lemon grass and ginger broth. The broth alone was so delicious that I spent 5 minutes sipping it from the side of the deep plate. Slow down and stay awhile in the family-friendly atmosphere, complete with a children's menu and larger tables for groups.

2129 Lake Placid Rd., Creekside. ✆ 604/932-4424. Reservations recommended. Main courses C$14.95–C$32.95 (US$9.35–US$21). Children's menu available. AE, MC, V. Weekdays 5:30pm–10pm, weekends 11pm.

Edgewater Lodge Lakeside Dining Room WEST COAST *(Finds*
You'll find Edgewater Lodge 5 minutes north of the Village, down a secluded lane to a pastoral waterfront setting. Candles are lit at your table and a pleasant murmur of conversation fills the 12-table room under a vaulted ceiling. In the small kitchen, executive chef Thomas Piekarski prepares his country cooking enhanced with garden vegetables and herbs. His passion for his menu has made him one of the top chefs in Whistler. The pan-seared camembert appetizer with mango chutney and fig compote was irresistible and a local favorite, along with Thomas's prawn bisque. Follow with a main course of venison medallions supplied by Lodge owner Jay Sullivan's ranch near Lillooet. Ask for the very lean venison served rare or medium rare, advises the chef. The breaded, stuffed, and baked chicken with roasted garlic is a filling dish, and you may end up taking some home. In winter, the room has a glowing warmth that feels light-years away from the bustle of Whistler Village. In summer, the late sunset highlights the view of Green Lake and a 180-degree vista from Whistler Mountain to Mt. Currie. Actor Tony Curtis once booked the entire restaurant for a party, and I could see why.

Head north of Whistler Village on Hwy. 99, turn right at the lights at Alpine Way, then take the first right. ✆ 888/870-9065, 604/932-0688. Reservations recommended. Main courses C$17.75–C$34.95 (US$11.10–US$21.85). AE, MC, V. Daily 6pm–9pm.

Evergreens Restaurant WEST COAST Newly renovated, Evergreens is a small, elegant affair. Occasionally, a pianist tinkles away at a grand piano, adding to the soignée atmosphere. Start with a great daily breakfast buffet or Sunday brunch, one of the best in Whistler. Move on to lunch or dinner, starting with appetizers such as a soup of mixed wild mushrooms with barley, garnished with Swiss chard, or roast butternut squash soup with spicy pecans and maple crème fraîche. The Taste of British Columbia Salmon is yummy, with three delicacies of salmon gravlax, smoked steelhead, and house-smoked salmon sushi-style roll. Your main choice might be tiger prawns and Pacific scallops, sautéed with smoked tomato cream, roasted shallots, arugula, and garganeli noodles. Venison striploin is served with sun-dried blueberry jus, wild rice, and pear chutney.

4050 Whistler Way, in the Delta Whistler Resort, Whistler Village. © 604/932-7346. Reservations recommended. Main courses C$20.95–C$32.95 (US$13.10–US$20.60). AE, DC, MC, V. Daily 6:30am–2pm, 5:30pm–10:30pm.

Trattoria di Umberto ITALIAN   Umberto Menghi added to his stable of posh Vancouver Italian restaurants by opening "The Trat" and its sister restaurant, Il Caminetto (4242 Village Stroll, © **604/932-4442**) in Whistler. Born in Pontedera, Tuscany, Umberto is an icon on the Canadian dining scene, with cookbooks, a television cooking show, and a cooking school in Tuscany to his credit. Today he owns seven West Coast restaurants in Vancouver and Whistler. Umberto's zest for the Tuscan cooking of his homeland infuses his menu. Banquettes, large convivial tables, and a long bar popular with diners seat a total of 120 guests. Antipasto Trattoria or beef Carpaccio with aromatic vegetables, capers, and Parmesan make good starters. Follow up with linguine, spaghetti, fettuccine, penne, tortellini, agnolotti, or cannelloni. Umbert's cioppino of mixed seafood in a light saffron, fennel, and tomato broth is his famously flavorful, feeds-more-than-one, main course soup dish. You can even take home a bottle of his own Tuscan hand-pressed extra virgin olive oil, C$20 (US$12.50).

4417 Sundial Place in the Mountainside Lodge, Whistler Village. © 604/932-5858. Reservations recommended. Main courses C$14.95–C$32.95 (US$9.35–US$20.60). AE, DC, MC, V. Daily noon–2:30pm, 5:30pm–10pm.

Zeuski's Taverna MEDITERRANEAN   Enjoy gracious Mediterranean dining with delightful and inventive creations on the lunch, dinner, and children's menus. Lunch could be a Kotapoulo burger of tender chicken breast rolled in pistachio nuts, topped with tzatziki, roasted red peppers, and feta cheese. Fresh falafel and wraps along with traditional souvlaki are authentically prepared. The food here is surprisingly light. Try the delicious Empire Salad, a pepper-crusted lamb sirloin nestled on fresh tomato slices and baby organic greens, topped with a chunk of goat feta, then drizzled with herbed Dijon vinaigrette. Kalamari (not breaded) is pan-seared in extra virgin olive oil, finished with fresh garlic, butter, and lemon, enchanting in its taste. Roasted lamb sirloin is stuffed with feta cheese, roasted red pepper, and garlic, drizzled with roasted garlic Merlot sauce and crowned with fresh rosemary. Desserts are made in-house, with traditional baklava layered with chopped pistachios, almonds, and walnuts—a sweet finish to a wonderful meal. On the children's menu all items are C$5 (US$3.10), including chicken fingers with fries or pizza with tomato sauce and cheese, and Jell-O for dessert.

40-4314 Main St., Village North. ℂ **604-932-6009.** Reservations recommended in high season. Main courses C$14–$C31 (US$8.75–US$19.35). AE, DC, MC, V. Daily 11:30am–11pm.

MODERATE

Brewhouse STEAK & PIZZA   Look for the clock tower to find Brewhouse. With a brewing facility upstairs (free tours Wed and Sat at 3pm with Master Brewer Pete Kis,toth) and a casual atmosphere overall, the two-level Brewhouse is a place for all ages. Located across from the new Maurice Young Millennium Theatre, Brewhouse features a wood-fired pizza oven and rotisserie out in the open where chefs dish up pizzas, prime rib, and fresh chicken. Lunch can be as simple as a Philly cheese steak sandwich or tuna melt. Dinner items include mixed mushroom pizza with fresh thyme and roasted garlic, as well as spit-roasted half chicken or spit-roasted Alberta grain-fed prime rib. Mountain fresh beers brewed in-house include Big Wolf Bitter, Dirty Miner Stout, Twin Peaks Pale Ale, Lifty Lager, Northern Light Lager, and Frank's Nut Brown Ale. The Brewhouse Pub is open until midnight. Sit at a window or out on the patio and watch the parade stroll through Village North.

4355 Blackcomb Way, Village North. ℂ **604/905-2739.** Reservations accepted. Main courses C$8.95–C$27.95 (US$5.60–US$17.45). Children's menu available. AE, MC, V. Daily 11:30am–10pm.

Caramba! Restaurante MEDITERRANEAN   A year-round local favorite, Caramba! was rated by Zagat as one of the top 10 most popular restaurants in Whistler. For a shot of high energy and a good deal year-round, this is the place, seating 150 inside and 100 outside on the patio. The very word *Caramba* means "Wow," and that sums up the atmosphere—busy, noisy, with fast service. The Mediterranean-influenced menu offers fresh ingredients, prepared with a great deal of pizzazz. Try the fettuccine Natasha with fresh

salmon and pepper vodka tomato cream sauce, the free-range rosemary chicken, or country-style pot roast. Or share a wood-burning,
oven-baked pizza, a plate of wood-fired penne, or grilled New York
steak. The restaurant's signature item is calamari à la Plancha, an
appetizer of fresh grilled squid served to the tune of 22 kilograms
(50 lb.) a day.

12-4314 Main St., Town Plaza, Village North. (C) **604/938-1879**. Main courses
C$12–C$20 (US$7.50–US$12.50). AE, MC, V. Lunch Fri–Sun 11:30am–5pm, daily
5pm–11pm.

The Crab Shack SEAFOOD, STEAKS   This casual eatery makes
you feel as if you're dining in the forest, although only steps away
from Highway 99. The breakfasts and lunches are a good deal, starting around C$5 (US$3.10). In the evening, the real draw is oysters
prepared by oyster shucker Chris Field, who serves up to five flavors
nightly raw on the half-shell. Eating oysters with Chris is like traveling Canada, with Malpeque oysters from Prince Edward Island to
Pearl Bay oysters from Sechelt, BC. *Note:* Chris started shucking
oysters in 1988, and advises that you chew them well. Slurping down
a partially chewed raw oyster is hard on the gastrointestinal system.

The Crab Shack also serves some high-end dainties, such as a whop-
ping New York steak with medallions of garlicked Caribbean lobster.
In the next room, a 130-seat lounge with sports on eight TVs broad-
casts NHL, NBA, and NFL action. At Wednesday jam nights, catch
live music with host Pete (of local Pete and Chad fame). On Sunday
night, Whistler's party band Whole Damn County blasts away and the
place is packed with folks indulging in mounds of 10¢ chicken wings.

4005 Whistler Way, across from Coast Whistler Hotel, Whistler Village. (C) **604/932-
4451**. Main courses C$9.95–C$50 (US$6.20–US$37.50). DC, DISC, MC, V. Daily
7am–11pm.

Les Deux Gros FRENCH COUNTRY *(Value*   Owner and chef
Pascal Tiphine reveals that he started life in Whistler as a ski bum in
1978 and has ended up king of his own 120-seat restaurant. His
establishment is a short cab ride from the Village, but for atmosphere
and originality, the few dollars are worth it. Set on a small hill surrounded by trees, this is the place to dawdle away a summer evening
over food and wine on the covered 60-seat balcony patio. In winter,
you can watch the snowflakes drift by the floor-to-ceiling windows.
Born in France and trained as a chef in Switzerland, Pascal incorpo-
rates the best of both cuisines into his menu with meat, game, and
poultry, as well as fish and seafood. Start with Mussels à la Pascal,
steak tartare, or Alsace onion pie. Move on to the rack of lamb

Whistler Valley Dining

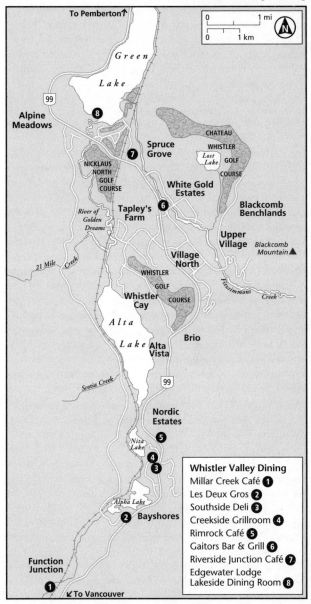

To Pemberton↑

Green Lake

99

Alpine Meadows

CHATEAU WHISTLER GOLF COURSE

Lost Lake

Spruce Grove

NICKLAUS NORTH GOLF COURSE

White Gold Estates

River of Golden Dreams

Blackcomb Benchlands

Tapley's Farm

Upper Village

Blackcomb Mountain ▲

21 Mile Creek

Village North

WHISTLER GOLF COURSE

Whistler Cay

Fitzsimmons Creek

Alta Lake

Alta Vista

Brio

Scotia Creek

99

Nordic Estates

Nita Lake

Alpha Lake

Bayshores

Function Junction

↙To Vancouver

Whistler Valley Dining
Millar Creek Café ❶
Les Deux Gros ❷
Southside Deli ❸
Creekside Grillroom ❹
Rimrock Café ❺
Gaitors Bar & Grill ❻
Riverside Junction Café ❼
Edgewater Lodge
Lakeside Dining Room ❽

diable, a succulent seven-chop rack roasted with Dijon mustard, or tiger prawns and scallops prepared with Indian-style curry. Rabbit, Viennaise Schnitzel, and wild BC sockeye salmon are also on the menu. For dessert, crème caramel or profiteroles au chocolat anyone? Prices are moderate for Whistler, but the food is quality. Children's menu. Ample free parking.

1200 Alta Lake Rd. Drive south of the Village until you see the Les Deux Gros sign at Alta Lake Rd. Turn right, then the first left. ℂ 604/932-4611. Reservations recommended. Main courses C$17.95–C$28.95 (US$11.25–US$18.10). AE, DC, MC, V. Daily 5:30pm–11pm.

Tex Corleone's BBQ, PIZZA   This Western-style restaurant takes a fun approach to chicken, ribs, and Chicago-style deep dish pizza that kids as well as adults find satisfying. Breakfast starts the day with a buffet or individual items. Lunch includes Thai chicken, and lunch spinach, a fine summer choice with caramelized pecans, hard-boiled eggs, and real crispy bacon tossed in a house-made Dijon vinaigrette. Try on the bronco beef ribs smothered in co-owner Li'l Joe Kovacks's famous apple barbecue sauce or chicken gravy. If that doesn't fill you up, the AAA prime Alberta beef ribs and rotisserie chicken combinations will feed at least two or more. Be prepared to wait 20 minutes for your mammoth Chicago deep-dish pizza. Thin-crust pizzas are also available. General manager Iona Lake is likely to be on hand to greet you and give the kids coloring pages, crayons, and cowboy hats to keep them amused. Just so you don't squeal "too much," it's best to take company along to Tex's. Free delivery on takeout orders.

4154 Village Green in Crystal Lodge, Whistler Village. ℂ 604/932-7427. Main courses C$14.95–C$27.95 (US$9.35–US$17.50). DC, MC, V. Daily 7am–11pm.

Thai One On THAI   Thai artifacts decorate this simple restaurant and set the tone for food that is a blend of Eastern and Western influences, focusing on color, taste, and aroma. Elegant dishes balance sweet, sour, salty, and spicy, the four pillars of Asian cooking. Many love hot Thai food, but if hot is not to your taste, ask for suggestions. Good here are satays, coconut prawns, and Pad Pak Nammun Hoi, a dish combining fresh spinach, tofu, garlic, peppers, and red onions fried in oyster sauce. Po Pia Tod is a golden-fried, flaky vegetable spring roll served with tangy sweet-and-sour sauce. As with Thailand itself, all food is artistic in its presentation, and a pleasure to behold. A cold Singha beer from Bangkok, Tsingtao from China, or Sapporo from Japan goes very well with any dish. A wine list is also available. The staff will happily wrap up your extras to take home. Delivery service is available.

108-4557 Blackcomb Way in Le Chamois, Upper Village. © **604/932-4822.**
Reservations recommended. Main courses C$11–C$22 (US$6.85–US$13.75). AE,
DC, MC, V. Daily 5pm–10pm. Complimentary underground parking.

Finds **The Bard Would Approve**

To beef pie or to chicken pie, that is the question.... The
Bard would approve of **Shakespeare's Pies,** 201-4000
Whistler Way above the Royal Bank Building in Whistler
Village (© **604/935-1743**). With several thousand Australians
living in Whistler, Douglas Taylor and his partners guessed
that launching a carbon copy of Sydney's Shakespeare's
Pies was a good bet. Their little bakery on the second floor
opened Australia Day, January 26, 2001, and caught on
with the locals right away. Join them while you munch on
your substantial mini-pie inside or outside on the balcony
picnic tables. These could really be the best pies on the
planet. Gourmet beef, chicken, or vegetarian savory versions, C$3.50 to C$4.50 (US$2.20 to US$2.80) are baked
almost round-the-clock with premium-quality ingredients,
no artificial colors, flavorings, MSG, or unbleached flour.
The biggest seller is a steak, potato, and cheese item similar to a shepherd's pie. None of the pies see a microwave,
and none are reheated. Sweet pies are numerous, with
strawberry-rhubarb crumble a sweet and tangy combination. Savory and sweet family-sized pies are available
cooked or uncooked for C$11.95 to C$18.95 (US$7.45 to
US$11.85). If you're staying in Whistler awhile, get your
"Frequent Piers" card stamped. After you buy 10 pies, you
get a two-for-one reward. Open daily from 9:30am to 3am.

---

3 Good Deals

Chef Bernard's FARM GATE CUISINE *Finds*   A love of produce
fresh from the fields of local suppliers inspired chef Bernard
Casavant to move on from the Fairmont Chateau Whistler to his
own tiny cafe in the shadow of his former employ. The chef is
co-chair of the local seasonal farmers market, so you can be sure
his produce is the height of freshness. In winter, he favors seasonal

winter root vegetables in unusual soups such as rutabaga and apple. In summer, salads and sauces are a forte with field lettuces, tomatoes, stone fruits, tree fruits, and berries as ingredients. At breakfast, order the griddle cakes with local berry sauce, or one of the best and sweetest cinnamon buns you'll ever eat. Later in the day, try hot entrees like chicken with penne. For a BC taste sensation, experience the speared wild sockeye salmon sandwich. Chef Bernard also promotes and supports all BC estate wineries. Next door is his 26-seat **BBK's Pub,** an intimate, popular adult spot for dinner, where the lights are set romantically low. Customers order in from Chef Bernard's next door. The Blackcomb Beer and Wine Store at the same location completes the chef's trio.

1-4573 Chateau Blvd., Whistler Village. © **604/932-7051.** Main courses C$16–19 (US$10–US$11.85). AE, MC, V. Daily 7am–9pm.

Esquires Coffee House PANINI CAFE FARE   Voted Whistler's best new coffee shop for 2001, the casual, art-filled Esquires serves up delicious Eggins, wonderful little broccoli and cheese quiches, and freshly built grilled panini and wraps, along with substantial gourmet soups. The eggnog latte is superb and smooth, and the fruit smoothies are blended on the spot in dairy or non-dairy versions. Kids and adults alike will swoon over the Italian sodas and the hand-packed milkshakes. Desserts are all made locally. You must try the NUMI teas, imaginative blends of whole-leaf teas and herbs; the Dry Lime is a tongue treat. Take some home. After an evening stroll through the village, stop in for hot cider or chocolate, with a biscotti or apricot square. Esquires can get very busy, but the graciousness of the staff makes the wait worth your while.

127-4338 Main St. (backside), Village North. © **604/905-3386.** Main courses C$1.50–C$5.95 (US$1–US$3.70). AE, DISC, MC, V. Open Mon–Sat 7am–10:30pm. Sun and holidays 8am–10pm.

Gaitors Bar & Grill SOUTHWESTERN   Located on the top floor over a pub at the Shoestring Lodge, Gaitors is funky, fun, and affordable. A 5-minute drive from the Village, Gaitors shares some of the laidback atmosphere of the Lodge itself, a magnet for low-rent skiers and snowboarders. Head here with your family for burgers (including a grilled tuna burger), veggie enchiladas, Thai curried prawns, and spicy Yucatan chicken lime soup. Go Mexican with beef and choose quesadilla, veggie burrito, or chicken chimichanga. Finish up with a specialty coffee and relax. It's allowed here. There's an all-day breakfast Saturday and Sunday with a Sunday brunch buffet as well.

7124 Nancy Greene Dr., north of Whistler Village. ✆ **604/938-5777**. Main courses C$9–C$17 (US$5.60–US$10.60). Children's menu available. AE, MC, V. Open weekdays 5:30pm–10:30pm, Satu–Sun 8am–10:30pm.

Old Spaghetti Factory ITALIAN   Furnished with warm wood antiques and staffed with genuinely friendly people, this is the best place for family meals. Entrees (children's menu, too) include minestrone soup or salad, sourdough bread, spumoni ice cream, tea and coffee. All sauces, dressings, and soups are prepared fresh daily. Fresh tortellini, lasagna, or spaghetti with tomato sauce, meat sauce, or clam sauce head up the menu. Grilled New York steak with heaps of sautéed mushrooms and spaghetti with tomato sauce is a hearty dinner. Veggie lasagna stuffed with four cheeses, green peppers, onions, carrots, spinach, and mushrooms topped with tomato sauce is a great choice. All the offerings are tasty and generous, and older family members can choose from the children's menu selections. To avoid a long wait, use the phone-ahead service after 5pm: call 1 hour ahead and you'll be placed on the list and informed of the length of your wait.

4154 Village Green in Crystal Lodge, Whistler Village. ✆ **604/938-1081**. Reservations requested for 6 or more in group. Main courses C$9–C$15 (US$5.60–US$9.35), children C$4.95–C$6.65 (US$3.10–US$4.15). AE, MC, V. Daily noon–9:30pm.

Pasta Lupino Gourmet ITALIAN *(Value (Finds*   Generous portions of freshly made pasta and sweetly fragrant sauces make Pasta Lupino a must. Owners Kendra and Kevin Mazzei received the local's Pasta of the Year award for their small, six-table restaurant. They show a keen appreciation of seasonal vegetables, ladling out roasted carrot and yam soup, followed with either a tangy traditional caesar salad (with garlic and anchovies) or a mixed green with pesto vinaigrette. The chicken parmigiana and fresh linguine showcases their cooking skill. Highly recommended is the lightly crumbed boneless chicken breast, moist and topped with fresh tomato and mozzarella cheese, served with linguine. A local's favorite is Pasta Rose, a blend of Alfredo sauce with fresh basil and tomato sauce on a choice of semolina radiatore or spinach caesar noodles. The tiny but tight wine list offers Summerhill Estate Winery Baco Noir 2000, a knowledgeable match with any of the pasta dishes. The tiramisu dessert is both heavenly and deadly at the same time. As a treat, take home some hand-packed Salt Spring Island chevre cheese. If you can't get in, order takeout, like many visitors and locals.

121-4368 Main St., beside 7-Eleven, Village North. ✆ **604/905-0400**. Reservations not accepted. Main courses C$10.95–C$13.95 (US$6.85–US$8.70). MC, V. Sun–Thurs 11am–9pm, Fri–Sat 11am–10pm.

Southside Deli BREAKFASTS & CAJUN   Some things never change, and that's a darn good thing. If you want a peek at what Whistler was like 20 years ago, stop in and say hi to Cal cooking his famous "Beltch" breakfast special of bacon, eggs, cheese, and ham on a beat-up griddle that still works like a charm. As proprietor of the oldest deli in Whistler, Cal has served over one million Eggs Bennies. In winter, the clientele prop their snowboards and skis on the tiny patio outside while they lunch on burgers, sandwiches, and soup, a mere 2-minute walk to the Creekside Gondola. One new addition, however, is Chef Steve Letts's Rajun Cajun menu, served from 5pm to 10pm, Thursday to Sunday. Steve's Cajun roots are on his mother's side, inspiring him to create Po'Boys with blackened snapper, BBQ charbroiled pork tenderloin with a mango and smoked chipotle sauce, and Cajun chicken burgers.

2102 Lake Placid Rd., Creekside. © **604-932-3368.** Main courses C$9–C$13 (US$5.60–US$8.10). AE, V. Mon–Wed 6am–3pm, Thurs–Sun 6am–10pm.

Splitz Grill BURGERS WRAPS *Kids*   Proud to be called Whistler's first and only true burger joint, Splitz is owned by Trevor and Miriam Jackson, a young couple who opened this expanded 60-seat space in June 2001, a step up from their former location with 10 seats. The new Splitz also has a liquor license. The grilled Splitz burger is 5 ounces of seasoned all-beef burger with a garlic and mayonnaise sauce, but you can also order a spicy lentil vegetarian burger. Add a side of fries, and an assortment of unusual fixings such as hummus, baba ganoush, and sauerkraut. To finish off (or finish you off) order a banana split drenched in warm caramel-coated bananas with three flavors of ice cream chosen from a palate of 12 flavors. Once you've had one, you'll know why some people go to Splitz strictly for the sugar rush.

4369 Main St. at Alpenglow Hotel, Village North. © **604/938-9300.** Main courses C$3.95–C$8.95 (US$2.45–US$5.60). Children's menu available. V. Daily 11am–10pm.

Uli's Flipside EUROPEAN   First opened in 1992 at Creekside, the ever-youthful Uli's Flipside is now in a second-floor location in Whistler Village just steps away from the Village Gondola. A best bet for late-night dining, Uli's promises good food, funky tunes, and local color, not to mention a moderately priced menu and wine list. The 140-seat room has a vaulted ceiling and window-side booths, with an upstairs loft seating 50 diners. Uli's is also the best bet for late-night dining. Recommended are schnitzel, chicken linguine, and spicy Italian salcsiccia sausage homemade by owner Uli Schnuur, then sautéed in spicy tomato cream sauce with penne pasta.

4433 Sundial Place in the St. Andrews building, Whistler Village. © **604/935-1107.** Main courses C$11.95–C$18.95 (US$7.45–US$11.85). MC, V. Mon–Sat 3pm–2am, Sun 3pm–midnight.

4 Quick Bites

Auntie Em's Kitchen (© **604/932-1163**) at 129-4340 Lorimer, Village North, is a 26-seat deli bakery with freshly ground espresso coffee and specialty lattes and cappuccinos for a quick pit stop. If you get up late, they serve breakfast all day. A good spot if you're a vegetarian, with one veggie special daily (such as homemade Hungarian goulash with Spatzl made from scratch) plus on-site baked European-style pastries, rye breads, soups, sandwiches, and salads. Eat in or take out daily from 6:30am to 6pm. Ample free parking at Whistler Marketplace.

Black's Original Ristorante (© **604/932-6408**) at 4270 Mountain Square, Whistler Village, base of the Whistler Village Gondola, is a quick-stop family restaurant for breakfast, lunch, and dinner. Fuel up with hand-tossed pizzas, many varieties of pastas, heaps of fries, and a choice of five "main event" dishes including AAA sirloin steak or chicken parmigiana. Pizza and main courses from C$10.95 to C$19.95 (US$6.85 to US$12.45). Open daily from 7am to 11pm.

Gone Bakery & Soup Company (© **604/905-4663**) is found at 4205 Village Square, Whistler Village. Step into Armchair Books and head for the back, where you'll find a tiny popular spot for breakfast, lunch, or dinner. Lunch for two can easily be done under C$20 (US$12.50) with curried beef and lentil soup, and a grilled veggie and goat cheese sandwich followed by home-cooked lemon square or pecan pie. Open daily from 6:30am to 9pm. Buy a loaf of sourdough and take it home.

Ingrid's Village Café (© **604/932-7000**) at 4305 Skier's Approach, next to the hardware store in Whistler Village, is open daily from 8am to 6:30pm. This is a local favorite for quality and price, and is especially good if you're a vegetarian. A veggie burger or veggie pie here will hardly make a dent in your wallet. Team up a garden rice-and-beans falafel with veggie barley soup, or a spanakopita or samosa with a corn and chicken chowder, and you've had a tasty, substantial lunch for under C$10 (US$6.25).

Millar Creek Café (© **604/938-1151**) at 1-1200 Alpha Lake Rd. is an accessible Function Junction cafe, with free parking and no hassles. Sit down with the locals for an easygoing breakfast fritatta or a lunch special such as chicken satay on a Greek pita, C$7.95 (US$4.95). Finish up with a sticky cinnamon bun baked on the premises. Open from 8am to 4pm weekdays; Saturday to Sunday from 9am to 4pm.

Riverside Junction Café (© **604/938-2933**) is located at 8018 Mons Rd. at the Riverside RV Resort and Campground. Turn right at Blackcomb Way 1.6km (1 mile) north of Whistler Village. Don't get the idea that a campground is no place to eat. The cafe is located in the Riverside RV Resort's impressively huge, new log cabin head-quarters. It's a friendly place to eat year-round, open daily from 7am to 9pm serving inexpensive all-day breakfasts and eat-until-you-drop lunches under C$8.95 (US$5.60). Dinner ranges from breaded veal schnitzel to New York steak with peppercorn sauce, C$14.95 to C$19.95 (US$9.35 to US$12.45). Specialty coffees and desserts also served. Free parking.

5 Asian

Amami Restaurant (© **604/932-6431**) at 4274 Mountain Square, second floor, near the Whistler Village Gondola, offers Chinese and Japanese items in a casual atmosphere, with free delivery on orders over $25. Average entree price is C$10 (US$6.25). Open from 11:30am to 2:30pm, 4:30pm to 10pm. Pick-up and delivery available.

Mongolie Grill (© **604/938-9416**) at 201-4295 Blackcomb Way near the Holiday Inn is an award-winning Chinese stir-fry restaurant for lunch and dinner. Fare is based on seafood, tender meats, and Asian noodles, accompanied by 18 gourmet sauces from around the world. The chef will stir-fry in front of your eyes. Food is sold by weight, C$3.10 (US$1.95) per 100 grams (3.52 oz.), averaging C$25 for a hungry adult. Lunch is 20% off year-round. In summer, enjoy the sun on the licensed patio. No reservations accepted. Open daily from 11:30am to 10:30pm.

Sushi Village (© **604/932-3330**) at 4272 Mountain Square, sec-ond floor, near the Whistler Village Gondola, is a very casual spot for Japanese cuisine, with lunch and dinner menus. A set dinner such as chicken teriyaki is C$25 (US$15.60), but many diners choose to order sushi, tempura, and other items a la carte. Open daily from 5pm to 10pm, Wednesday to Sunday noon to 2:30pm for lunch. Reservations requested for four or more.

Tandoori Grill (© **604/905-4900**) at 201-4368 Main St., Village North, is the only Whistler restaurant offering authentic East Indian cuisine. Dishes are as mild or as hot as you request, with seasonings like fresh ginger, fresh garlic, dry coriander, cilantro, onions, tomatoes, and fenugreek. Butter chicken is popular, marinated in ginger and garlic. Another favorite is palak paneer, fresh spinach cooked in ginger, garlic, and onions with homemade cheese. Prices range from C$9.95 to C$16.95 (US$6.20 to US$10.60). Reservations recommended. Open from 12pm to 3pm, 5pm to 11pm. Takeout and delivery available.

Teppan Village Japanese Steak House (© **604/932-2223**) at 4291 Mountain Square in the Delta Whistler Resort, Whistler Village, is the place to be entertained by dexterous chefs and their flashing knives carving up your meal at this teppan-yaki-style restaurant. The specialty is steak, but chicken and seafood are available. The atmosphere is a little more upscale than casual, but still relaxed and fun. Reservations suggested in peak seasons. Open from 5:30pm to 10pm. Dinner is in the C$22 to C$52 (US$13.75 to US$32.50) range.

Whistler Noodle House (© **604/932-2228**) is located at 3-4330 Northland Blvd., Whistler Marketplace, Village North. A standard Chinese restaurant with a large menu of mix-and-match dishes from C$5.95 to C$14.95 (US$3.70 to US$9.35), it features soups, noodles, chow mein, fried rice, chicken, duck, seafood, pork, beef, and vegetarian ingredients. Special combinations take the guesswork out of ordering, starting at C$44.95 (US$28.10) for dinner for two. Open daily from 11am to 9pm. Free parking. Free delivery on takeout orders of C$40 (US$25) or more.

5

Whistler in Winter

Whistler winter activities really kick off when Whistler and Blackcomb mountains open on the US Thanksgiving weekend. More than 2.5 million skier visits were recorded in the 2000–2001 season (which you could argue lasts as long as 8 months, if you count summer skiing on Blackcomb's Horstman Glacier). And if you're not into downhill skiing or snowboarding, you can try cross-country skiing, snowmobiling, heli-skiing, heli-snowboarding, snowshoeing, sleigh rides, dog sledding, and much more.

So what do you do in Whistler in winter if you're not the active sporty type? The resort is also a good place to relax, go shopping, read books, visit the Whistler Museum & Archives, swim in the outdoor hotel pools or the indoor Meadow Park Athletic Centre before heading to a restaurant or club (see chapter 4, "Where to Dine," and chapter 8, "Whistler After Dark"). Stroll around the resort, talk to people, buy groceries, and cook your own meals in your condo. If you have the impression that Whistler is all hustle and bustle, you'll be surprised at how peaceful being in a mountain getaway can be.

One good way to plan activities is to contact **Tourism Whistler,** the resort's official reservation service (4010 Whistler Way, Whistler, BC V0N 1B4, *✆* **800/944-7853** in the US and Canada, www.tourism whistler.com) for customized activity planning and packages including lift tickets. Call for brochures, general resort information, activities and events, snow conditions, highway information, and the weather. Tourism Whistler represents the majority of local activity providers, and can book everything from skiing and snowboarding to dog sledding and snowmobile rides. You can also visit Tourism Whistler's offices located just off Village Gate Boulevard in the Whistler Conference Centre, Whistler Village.

For anything to do with Whistler and Blackcomb mountains, such as lift tickets and advice on skiing, snowboarding, lessons, and rentals, you can also contact **Whistler/Blackcomb Mountain** (4545 Blackcomb Way, Whistler, BC V0N 1B4, *✆* **800/766-0449,**

604/932-3434, www.whistler-blackcomb.com). The website is a good way to get to know the mountain activities.

You can also contact individual activity providers by calling the telephone numbers noted in "Other Activities" later in this chapter. Quite a few companies also act as activity brokers, so this is another way to go.

Tips Snow Report

For a free up-to-date **snow report from Whistler/Blackcomb,** call © **604/687-7507** in Vancouver, © **604/932-4211** in Whistler. Updated daily at 6am and 3:30pm, you'll hear the current temperatures in Whistler Village and the alpine conditions on the mountains, snowfall information, snow base, wind conditions, weather forecast, and next-day snow report.

---

1 The Dual Mountains

The dual mountains of **Whistler and Blackcomb** are the unbeatable reason why Whistler Resort is voted number one in North America year after year. Why is Whistler such a draw? Over and over visitors say that the mountains are "huge," an awesome hugeness that is both thrilling and intimidating.

Blackcomb rises to 1,609m (5,280 ft.), and this "magic mile" makes it the highest vertical in North America. Whistler Mountain at 1,530m (5,020 ft.) is the second highest. The longest run on each mountain is a thrilling, satisfying 11km (7 miles). With a total of 7,071 acres of skiable terrain, novice, intermediate, and expert skiers find plenty to experience. There are more than 200 runs, not to mention "a handful of insane 52-degree couloirs," as one writer put it. If you're a novice, the green runs from the tops of both Whistler and Blackcomb will rapidly improve your skills (or convince you to never ski again). More than 90 runs are groomed nightly on average, which gives the mountains the most groomed terrain of virtually any ski resort in North America.

Visitors also like the convenience of the extensive lift system, which is capable of carrying 26,295 skiers and snowboarders per hour on Whistler and 29,112 per hour on Blackcomb. With 15 high-speed lifts (out of a 33-lift system), Whistler/Blackcomb boasts the most high-speed lifts at a single resort in North America. Once you're up on the mountains, you can ski marked trails, steep powder chutes, challenging mogul fields, secluded tree ski areas, and groomed cruising runs. You can also play in 12 bowls and three glaciers.

Snowboarding is now almost as popular as skiing. Early on, Blackcomb Mountain was savvy enough to recognize that the sport wasn't going to go away and made space for it accordingly. Today Whistler/Blackcomb is seeing the results. Four major snowboarding competitions take place here each year, attracting competitors from around the world. For more on snowboarding, see "Snowboarding Reigns" below.

WHISTLER MOUNTAIN

Thirty-five years have made a tremendous difference to London Mountain. For one thing, it's now known as Whistler Mountain, a name with far more panache.

Fun Fact   From 3 Days to 120 Minutes

In the beginning, the journey to Whistler took 3 days—a steamer-ship ride from Vancouver to Squamish, overnight in Brackendale, and a 2-day horse trek up the Pemberton Trail. Then, in 1914, the Pacific Great Eastern Railway, now BC Rail, reached Alta Lake and opened up the valley to the outside world.

The Garibaldi Lift Company, with Franz Wilhelmsen as president, was formed in 1962 in order to erect and operate lifts on Whistler Mountain. By the fall of 1965 there was a four-person gondola to the mountain's mid-station, a double chairlift to the treeline, and two T-bars along with a day lodge. Whistler Mountain opened to the public in 1966, followed by Blackcomb Mountain in the winter of 1980–81, creating one of the largest ski complexes in North America. Whistler and Blackcomb mountains merged in 1996 under Intrawest Corporation.

By 1999 the community's permanent population had hit 9,000. Whistler now has the greatest number of ski-in/ski-out accommodations of any mountain recreation resort in North America.

Whistler Mountain has over 100 marked runs serviced by two high-speed gondolas, six high-speed quads, two triple chairs, one double chair, and five surface lifts. The mountain offers 3,657 acres of skiable terrain, with 20% designed for beginners, 55% for intermediate skiers, and 25% for advanced to expert skiers.

BLACKCOMB MOUNTAIN

Blackcomb's nickname is the Mile-High Mountain. It has over 100 marked runs serviced by one high-speed gondola, six high-speed quads, three triple chairs, and seven surface lifts. The mountain offers 3,414 acres of skiable terrain, with 15% designed for beginners, 55% for intermediate skiers, and 30% for the advanced and expert group. Summer skiing and training on Horstman Glacier continues well into August.

A few seasons back the mountain unveiled its superb Excalibur gondola system, featuring 97 eight-passenger sit-down cabins capable of carrying 2,600 skiers an hour. Combined with the Excelerator high-speed quad chair and the Glacier Express, skiers can climb from village to glaciers in 19 minutes.

2 Getting to Know the Mountains

When you can ski from any one of six mountain bases, choice is the name of the game.

Whistler Creekside Base offers convenient free parking close to the lifts in the day lots (entrance via Lorimer Rd.). Ride the six-passenger Creekside Gondola and Big Red Express quad to the top of Whistler Mountain. From here, you can take Harmony Express or The Peak, which carry skiers and riders to seven wide-open alpine bowls at both Little Whistler Peak at 2,115m (6,939 ft.) and Whistler Peak at 2,182m (7,160 ft.).

Whistler's Village Base features the 10-passenger high-speed Whistler Village Gondola rising 1,850m (6,069 ft.) to Roundhouse Lodge in the alpine. From here it's just one lift ride (The Peak) to the high alpine and seven bowls. **Fitzsimmons Express,** the newest Village Base lift, connects with Garbanzo Express to take you to Whistler Mountain's north-facing slopes, historically known as the Garbanzo Basin.

Blackcomb Mountain is accessed by the eight-passenger **Excalibur Gondola,** also leaving from the Whistler Village Base. Another route up Blackcomb is by way of **Excalibur Base II.** To get there, drive up Blackcomb Way past the bus loop, then make the

Whistler Blackcomb Mountains

courtesy of Whistler Blackcomb

first right at Glacier Drive and continue along the winding road to the free parking lot at the top. From here you can board Excalibur Gondola at mid-station and connect to Excelerator, which, after a short ski, will get you to the base of Glacier Express on Blackcomb Mountain. Finally, there is the accessible **Upper Village Blackcomb Base,** near the Fairmont Chateau Whistler. From here, skiers can take two high-speed quad chairs, the Wizard and Solar Coaster, to The Rendezvous at 1,860m (6,102 ft.). A third express lift will take you to the top of Seventh Heaven and Horstman Glacier, 2,284m (7,494 ft.) above the Village.

Tips Convenient Meeting Places

Set a meeting place and time for your group in case you get split up. Remember, the mountains are huge! Each mountain has meeting places with message boards in the alpine. Blackcomb Mountain has two meeting places: the light board at The Rendezvous and at Glacier Creek. On Whistler Mountain, meet at the Guest Satisfaction Centre Light Board near Round-house Lodge.

GETTING TO KNOW THE RUNS

Easiest Runs   Two mountains may seem like too much if you're just getting started, so start slow and warm up to the task. The entire area around Olympic Station on Whistler Mountain is specially tailored for learning. It's a slow-skiing zone with its own lifts and a Children's Learning Centre. From there, move over to the new Green Acres Family Zone off the Emerald Express, a good place to get your ski legs at the start of your day. On Blackcomb Mountain, beginners and kids start at the Magic Chair. Once you're warmed up, favorites include Easy Out from Expressway on Blackcomb and Lower Whiskey Jack off the Emerald Express on Whistler Mountain.

Intermediate Runs   With this much terrain it's hard to pick favorites. Blackcomb Mountain has lots of fall-line intermediate skiing and riding, especially in the Solar Coaster and Crystal Chair areas. Runs to try include Panorama on Seventh Heaven and Ridge Runner off Crystal Chair. On Whistler Mountain, try the Emerald

Express area for tree skiing or Harmony and Symphony Bowls to test your high-alpine off-piste skills. Grooming maps located at the base areas and key lifts of each mountain will lead you to the corduroy of the day.

Expert Runs   If you're comfy on black diamond runs and better, you'll no doubt have fun just finding your own way around. On Blackcomb Mountain, visit Spanky's Ladder. A short boot-pack up over the ridge brings you to Sapphire, Garnet, Diamond, and Ruby Bowls—site of the 2002 Extreme Skiing Championships. Davies Dirvish is Blackcomb's notorious double black diamond mogul run. On Whistler Mountain, the whole Harmony Ridge area shelters cool powder from the sun. The Peak chair will take you as high as it goes. Try to befriend a local to show you some secrets here. Whistler Bowl gives you the most vertical, and West Bowl keeps powder longer.

TICKET OPTIONS

Winter lift tickets are C$63 (US$39.35) for adults 19 to 64, C$54 (US$33.75) for youths 13 to 18, and C$32 (US$20) for children under 12 and seniors. A variety of multi-day passes is also available. Lifts are open daily from 8:30am to 3:30pm (and to 4:30pm from mid-March until closing, depending on weather and conditions). Since Whistler and Blackcomb mountains are jointly operated by Intrawest, your pass will give you dual access.

A 6-day ski pass is C$360 (US$225) for adults, C$295 (US$184.35) for youth, and C$173 (US$108) for children under 12 and seniors, significantly less expensive than 11 other major ski resorts, including Vail and Aspen.

Value Free Mountain Tours

Follow a local and get your bearings: free mountain tours are offered at 11:30am daily for intermediate and expert skiers. The Whistler Mountain Orientation Tour starts from the Guest Satisfaction Centre, under the light board at the top of the Whistler Village Gondola. The Blackcomb Mountain Orientation Tour starts from the Mountain Tour Centre at the top of the Solar Coaster Express. The Blackcomb Glacier Tour starts from the Mountain Tour Centre at the top of the Solar Coaster Express, weather permitting.

---

3 Ski Lessons & Ski Guides

WHISTLER AND BLACKCOMB SKI SCHOOL

Wherever you fit into the mountain scheme, there are lessons available to improve your skills and make your time on the mountain more enjoyable. From my own experience as a novice skier, I can guarantee that you'll feel more confident with even a half-day lesson on either mountain. You can **rent ski and snowboard gear** before purchasing your lift pass.

LESSONS AND MORE

Learn to Ski Programs   Start with this relaxed, beginner-only ski program from one afternoon to 3-day sessions. Monday and Friday starts include video and après. Prices range from C$95 (US$59.35) to C$315 (US$196.85). Meet at 9:45am and 12:30pm at Whistler Village Base and Blackcomb Base, respectively.

Private Lessons   Go one-on-one with your own professional, or make a private group with up to five family or friends. Half-day C$365 (US$228), full day C$545 (US$340).

Rossignol Daily Improvement Workshops   Improve your style and confidence and obtain tips on conditions and terrain, including video and Rossignol demo skis on Thursday and Friday sessions. Full day C$115 (US$71.85), afternoon C$95 (US$60). Whistler Mountain only. Meet at 9:45am and 12:45pm at Whistler Mountain top.

Super Group   Small intimate groups combine intense learning with social interaction. Limited to three students at the intermediate or expert levels. Includes videos. Sessions Sunday, Wednesday, and Friday. Half day C$129 (US$70.55), full day C$219 (US$136.85). Only on Blackcomb Mountain. Meet at 9:45am and 12:45pm at Blackcomb Mountain top.

MOUNTAIN EXPLORATION PROGRAMS

Ski and Ride Esprit   With skiers and riders of similar abilities from around the world, enjoy video analysis, a fun race, and daily après ski. Alumni from the program return year after year to explore the mountains. Four-day programs start Mondays, and 3-day programs start Fridays. Ride Esprit is available for snowboarders, offering the same format, pricing, meeting times, and locations. The 3-day program costs C$269 (US$168), and the 4-day program is C$299 (US$186.85). Meet at 8:45am at Garibaldi Lift Co. patio.

FREESKIING AND PERFORMANCE PROGRAMS

Atomic Dave Murray Ski Camp   One of the world's best camps combines gate training with all-mountain skiing. Tom Prochazka and his team of top coaches help turn out highly skilled, confident skiers year after year. Test-drive the latest Atomic demo skis, enjoy expert video analysis, a continental breakfast, slope-side snacks, great prizes, and après ski. The 3-day camps are C$399 (US$249). Meet at 8:30am at Garibaldi Lift Co. patio.

Atomic Gatebusters ℂ **800/766-0449**   A no-frills gate-training program for skiers with previous gate experience. Drop in for a day or purchase a pass for unlimited training (select Wed and Sat). A half-day is C$20 (US$12.50), a full day is C$33 (US$20.60), and a season pass is C$330 (US$206). Various dates. Meet on Whistler Mountain at the Whistler Race Centre and on Blackcomb Mountain on Ross's Gold.

Backcountry Adventures   Venture outside the Ski Area Boundary with a professional guide for a full day of serious vertical and a true taste of Coastal powder. No backcountry experience necessary. Minimum two people. The 1-day fee is C$150 (US$93.75). Meet at 8:30am at Essentially Blackcomb patio.

Extremely Canadian Freeskiing Clinics   Refine your off-piste techniques with top guides on some of the most challenging terrain in North America. The clinics include video analysis and a legendary après session at Merlin's. The 2-day clinic is C$329 (US$205), and the 4-day camp is C$599 (US$349). Meet at 8:30am at Essentially Blackcomb patio.

Ombrelle Stephanie Sloan Women Only Ski Program ℂ **900/766-0449**   This program was developed by a former World Champion Freestyle skier. Top female coaches share their secrets in bumps, steeps, and powder on Whistler Mountain. The program includes bump and powder clinics, video analysis, après ski, fun race, and wrap-up gourmet picnic. The 3-day clinic is C$269 (US$168), and the 1-day clinic is C$119 (US$74.35). Various dates.

Telemark Clinics   Try a 1-day introductory/beginner telemark clinic for C$99 (US$61.85), or a 2-day intermediate/advanced clinic for $C299 (US$186.85).

SMART MOGUL SKIING SPRING SESSIONS

Run independently by **SMS Camps Clothing** (ℂ **604/905-4421,** www.smartmogul.com) on Blackcomb or Whistler mountain (depending on which has the best snow available) and taught by World Cup skiers, these sessions will help you unlock the simple secrets of mogul skiing. If you're an intermediate adult to an up-and-coming competitor, the spring mogul sessions will enhance your range of motion and versatility. The director is John Smart, a two-time Olympian, 13-time World Cup medalist, and professional mogul champ. The camps have operated for more than a decade. One- to 3-day sessions are available, from mid-March to mid-April, for C$150 (US$93.75) to C$390 (US$243.75).

4 Snowboarding Reigns

Blackcomb Mountain jumped on the snowboarding bandwagon at least a decade ago, and has never looked back (see below). It's now considered to be the industry leader. Not only does it have a half-pipe, along with a variety of hits, rails, boxes, and jumps of all sizes, it boasts an epic sound system to boot. Whistler Mountain took a little longer to figure out the snowboarding phenomenon but now welcomes boarders with its own halfpipe. Seventy percent of the boarding facilities are rated intermediate. Check out the excellent map at www.whistlerblackcomb.com.

Blackcomb Mountain   The **Blackcomb Nintendo GAMECUBE Terrain Park** is three parks in one. The **Choker Terrain Park** is rated intermediate and includes features and jibs similar to those in the Highest Level Terrain Park, but smaller and not as advanced. Also contained here is the Snowcross Track, an area for intermediate to expert users to improve their racing and all mountain-freeriding skills. The **World Cup Halfpipe** on Blackcomb Mountain is designed for advanced to expert users, surrounded by trees, and has a permanent in-ground shape on a pitch of 17 degrees. The new **Highest Level Terrain Park** is located under the lower section of Catskinner Chairlift, and runs from above the DJ Shack to the bottom of the chairlift. Highest Level is split in half, with the left side rated double black diamond for experts and the right side rated black diamond for advanced users. Highest Level is huge and includes advanced and expert tabletops, hips, spines, and hike a rail sections. The rails and jibs in Highest Level are the most difficult, and designed to meet the needs of enthusiasts who are at the top of their game. Highest Level is enclosed by a permanent fence with access only through the top entrance. Riders/skiers must sign a waiver to obtain a C$15 (US$9.35) park pass, which is checked at the entrance prior to each entry. Helmets are mandatory in this area. Teens under 19 must bring a waiver signed by a parent or guardian.

Whistler Mountain The **Whistler Nintendo GAMECUBE Halfpipe** is located off the Emerald Express. It's great for intermediate and recreational users.

ADULT SNOWBOARD SCHOOL
Phone **Whistler Blackcomb Guest Relations** at ℂ **604/932-3434** for more details on the programs offered below.

Freestyle Private Lessons For intermediate to advanced snowboarders, these lessons are the easiest way to learn the skills needed to ride halfpipes and snowboard parks. They include video analysis. Two-hour lessons are C$239 (US$150).

Finds **Unique Snowboards Made in Canada**

Thirty World Cup medals have been won by athletes riding custom-built snowboards from Prior Snowboards of Whistler. Founder Chris Prior continues to handcraft distinctive and innovative boards, ranging from C$690 (US$431) to C$1,800 (US$1,125). Mark Fawcett won the 2000 ISF World Cup on a Prior Snowboard now prominently displayed in the showroom. Distinctly Canadian, the cores are made from aspen and birch grown in the province of Quebec. Topsheets are designed by local artist Chili Thom and feature Black Tusk, the Canadian flag, and designs of your choice. Models include men's and women's freeride boards, and a slope style freeride technical board. A neat innovation is The Backcountry split board, C$1,060 (US$662.50), which is perfect for telemark access to virgin snow off the beaten track. Using Volle top-grade hardware, the board can be split in half to ski in, then snapped back into one piece for an awesome descent.

US residents can have their board shipped directly back home, tax- and duty-free. Contact Prior Snowboard Manufactory Ltd., 5-1365 Alpha Lake Rd., Whistler, BC V0N 1B1, ℂ **877/937-7467**, 604/935-1923, fax 604/935-1924, www.priorsnowboards.com.

Learn to Ride Learn to snowboard in a relaxed environment on gently sloped beginner's areas. The school's unique teaching approach keeps you moving as you gradually progress from sliding to turning. Lessons feature specially designed Burton LTR snowboards. Prices range from C$73 (US$45.60) for an afternoon lesson to C$285 (US$178.10) for a 3-day lesson, lift, and rental. Meet at 10am and 12:45pm at Blackcomb Mountain, at Monk's Grill patio. For Whistler Mountain, meet in front of the Village Gondola building.

Mountain-Top Riding Clinics Choose your weapons and improve your riding with clinics in park and pipe, snowboard-cross, freeride, or carving. Afternoon sessions are C$83 (US$51.85); full-day sessions are C$93 (US$58.10). Meet at 10am and 12:45pm at Whistler Mountain top.

Private Lessons With your own professional coach, you choose the goals, the terrain, and the pace. Private lessons can be booked for one person or up to five people of similar snowboarding ability. Lift line priority. Full day is C$489 (US$305.60), 2-hour lessons (afternoons only) are C$239 (US$149.35).

MULTI-DAY PROGRAMS

Ride Esprit "Improve while you move" in Whistler/Blackcomb's popular mountain exploration program. Three to 4 days of mountain guiding, instruction, and fun. Includes video analysis, a fun race, lift line priority, and après receptions. Prices from C$259 (US$161).

Roxy Women's All-Star Snowboard Camps ⓒ 800/766-0449 These 2-day camps are coached by women for women for all levels of snowboard enthusiasts. The camp includes guided instruction, video analysis, après reception, equipment session, and prizes. Various dates. C$199 (US$124.35). A package including lift tickets is also available.

ⓕFinds **What About the Kids?**

Whistler Mountain is now home to the resort's first Family Zone, in Green Acres off the Emerald Express. Similar to a traffic school zone, the Family Zone features a large slow-skiing and boarding area ideal for families and for the first warm-up runs of any winter vacation. The area allows skiers and snowboarders to descend at a slower pace so that they can increase their experience and build confidence.

5 Visitors with Disabilities

The **Whistler Adaptive Ski Program** (© **800/766-0449, ext. 2071,** 604/905-2071, adaptiveski@intrawest.com) makes skiing accessible to everyone regardless of ability or challenges. Safety, enjoyment, and learning are top priorities. The program offers ski experiences on Whistler and Blackcomb mountains with equipment and facilities that cater to people with disabilities. Lifts on each mountain are accessible.

Safety First

Every year, people are seriously injured and even die on the mountains. For safety's sake, Ski Patrol offers this advice: Do not ski or ride alone. Watch for changing conditions, natural or manmade. Trail and slope conditions vary constantly with weather changes and usage. If you get lost or injured outside the ski area boundaries, you'll be on the hook for any rescue expenses incurred.

Fast, reckless, irresponsible, discourteous skiing or riding on any part of the mountain may result in loss of lift access privileges. Know the code, and ski with care.

Whistler/Blackcomb encourages the use of helmets for the sports of alpine skiing and snowboarding.

Observe all advisory signs. Ski and ride with care through all snowmaking areas, and be prepared to avoid snow vehicles and other manmade or natural obstacles. Ski and snowboard in a safe and controlled manner. If you have any questions or concerns regarding closures, safety, or terrain, talk to Ski Patrol members. If you see an accident on the hill that requires first aid, cross skis above the location and report the exact location and type of injury to the nearest mountain staff.

Programs are directed toward all abilities, from the beginner needing instruction to the seasoned skier needing only a guide and fresh powder. The Whistler Adaptive Ski Program is part of the Disabled Skiers Association of British Columbia, a not-for-profit organization. Together they provide an inventory of equipment featuring mono skis, bi-skis, three- and four-track equipment, and additional adaptive devices. Instructors and volunteers are certified by the Canadian Association of Disabled Skiers. They use the latest in adaptive skiing techniques to teach downhill skiing, snowboarding, and cross-country skiing to individuals and groups.

6 Other Winter Pursuits

CROSS-COUNTRY SKIING

Whistler Resort has a variety of backcountry, alpine, and valley Nordic ski opportunities, including the 30km (18.6 mile) Lost Lake Cross Country Trail system through diverse and scenic terrain. The patrolled trails are groomed and track set for both ski skating and touring, and feature a cozy log warming-hut on the shore of Lost Lake. For your added enjoyment, the 4km (2.4 miles) of trails that loop around Lost Lake are lit from 4pm to 10:30pm.

You can access the trails in two ways. Park in Whistler's free day lot 4A, cross the footbridge, and you'll find yourself at the Lost Lake Ticket Booth. Meadow Park Sports Centre, 5km (3.1 miles) north of the Village on Highway 99, is another starting point with ticket sales. Call ✆ **604/935-7529** and press 2 for grooming and weather conditions related to the cross-country trails, updated daily.

A 1-day pass for C$10 (US$6.25) and a book of 10 tickets for C$80 (US$50) are available. An Ultra Ski pass for C$13 (US$8.10) lets you use Meadow Park's hot tub, steam room, sauna, and pool. **Lost Lake Cross Country Connection** (✆ **604/905-0071,** www. crosscountryconnection.bc.ca), near the Lost Lake Ticket Booth, has lessons and rentals. **Whistler X-Country Ski & Hike** (✆ **888/ 771-2382,** 604/932-7711, www.whistlernordiccentre.com) offers lessons, rentals, tours, and backcountry skiing. Owner and director Savio Otis is a level IV instructor and former member of the Canadian Interski Demo Team. Activities are at the Nicklaus North Golf Club, with free transportation from and to your Whistler accommodation. Free parking is also available. **Whistler Wheel & Free Heel** (✆ **604/938-0898**) at Riverside RV Resort and Campground also gives lessons.

THE LOST LAKE TRAIL SYSTEM

Seven cross-country ski trails make up the Lost Lake trail system. Two additional trails can be found on the Fairmont Chateau Whistler Golf Course, and four more are located on the Nicklaus North Golf Course.

Chateau Whistler Golf Course Trails   The Upper Fairway is a gradual 2.3km (1.4 mile) uphill climb with views of southern mountains and Whistler Valley. The Black Loop Trail, affectionately known as Cardiac Hill, is a 2km (1.2 mile) big uphill climb with a winding steep downhill. Definitely not a good choice for beginners.

Dogsledding Basics

You may have seen sledding on TV, but nothing compares to being greeted by dozens of howling dogs anxious to get on with pulling you through the backcountry. **Cougar Mountain at Whistler** (© 604/932-4086, www.cougar mountain.ca) picks you up at 36-4314 Main St. in Village North and drives you some 20 minutes up a rough-hewn logging road, stopping briefly to attach chains to your vehicle. By the time you get to the warming hut, you feel like Sargeant Preston of the Northwest Mounted Police. The 90-minute sled ride through the Soo Valley Wildlife Reserve will delight any child who enjoys animals. They might even find themselves mushing their seven-dog sled under the watchful eye of the guide.

Tips to remember when you're driving a dog sled: Watch out if a lead dog starts to glance back. It may mean that members of the team aren't pulling their weight and that's one thing these hard-working dogs can't abide. After the run, throw a little raw chicken in their water. It gets the dogs drinking and prevents them from becoming dehydrated. You'll learn these and many more tips on your sled ride. Cost is C$125 (US$78) per person based on two passengers in the comfortable gondola-like sled.

Lost Lake   The Lost Lake Loop is a 1.8km (1 mile) beginner's favorite, an easy loop around the lake starting at the Warming Hut. The full Lost Lake Loop is 3.5km (2.1 miles), also an easy loop that starts at the Ticket Booth and includes the lake loop. The Centennial trail is a fun, rollercoaster ride of a trail that's 2.6km (1.6 miles) long. Vimy Ridge at .5km (.9 mile) is a flat cut-off trail that leads quickly to the Warming Hut. The Beach Cut at .3km (.1 mile) runs along the lake edge and continues onto the Lost Lake Loop. The 2km (1.2 mile) main connector trail from the northern routes back to Lost Lake is known as Old Mill Road. Dry Creek is the .4km (.2 mile) access route from Whistler Village to the main entrance to the Lost Lake trails. Upper Panorama is a 1.3km (.8 mile) steep uphill trail with great views of Lost Lake. Lower Panorama is a popular 2km (1.2 mile) intermediate trail rolling through cedar and fir forest.

Nicklaus North Golf Course Trails　You get big sky and beautiful open views from these valley floor trails. The Green Lake Loop is 2.5km (1.5 miles), Bear Trail is .6km (.3 mile), Bearberry Trail is 2.5km (1.5 miles), and Habitat Hollow is .3km (.1 mile).

HELI-SKIING

Are you good enough to take on the ultimate ski experience? If you're an intermediate or advanced skier or boarder yearning to suck up fresh powder, **Whistler Heli-Skiing** (© **888/HELISKI** or 604/932-4105; www.heliskiwhistler.com) is an established operator. Bell 212 twin-engine helicopters take you aloft for a three-run day, with 1,371 to 1,838m (4,500 to 6,000 vertical ft.) of skiing for C$560 (US$350) per person. A four-run day for expert skiers and boarders only, with 3,048 to 7,500m (10,000 to 12,000 vertical ft.) of skiing, is C$630 (US$393) per person, including a guide and lunch. Heli-skiing is for the fit, not the faint of heart. Snowboard and powder ski rentals run from C$35 (US$21.85) per day.

SLEIGH RIDES

For an old-fashioned sleigh ride, snuggle up in blankets with a number of good companies, each with its own specialty. You might get unflappable Tom and Jerry pulling your sleigh with **Blackcomb Horsedrawn Sleighrides** (© **604/932-7631,** www.blackcomb sleighrides.com). Owners Brian and Susan Clayton are the only ones licensed to conduct sleigh rides on Blackcomb Mountain, starting at Excalibur Base II. First you ride through a forested trail, then stop at a rustic cabin for a singing cowboy show and hot chocolate. Sounds corny and it is, but darn it's neat, especially with Whistler's lights twinkling below and a sky full of stars above. Sit in the back seats of the sleigh if you can. Those bags hanging from the horses' rears are there for a reason and if nature calls, the fumes are strong. Tours go out every evening and cost C$45 (US$28) for adults, C$35 (US$22) for 13- to 18-year-olds, and C$25 (US$15.60) for ages 3 to 12. Free under 3. Departures hourly from 5pm to 8pm.

For a ride around Green Lake, join **Whistler Outdoor Experience** (© **877/386-1888,** 604/932-3389, www.whistlerout door.com). Shaggy Malamute Stowie will welcome you, and may even come along for the 1-hour ride. Belgian Draft horses pull the sleigh through a snow-covered forest and along the shores of picturesque Green Lake, complete with warm blankets and hot beverages. You also get to see the row of massive million-dollar log mansions built overlooking the lake. Great fun for the whole family, at C$40 (US$25) for adults, C$20 (US$12.50) for those 12 and under. Free under 2. Daily sleigh rides leave on the hour from noon to 8 pm. Located at the 45-acre Edgewater Outdoor Centre, 3km (1.8 miles) north of Whistler Village.

Moments **Communing with the Stars**

If you find hurtling down a mountain on a snowmobile a little too unnerving, Canadian Snowmobile Adventures (© **604/938-1616,** www.cdn-snowmobile.com) also offers a SnowCat version of the same tour for C$129 (US$80.60). The spacious SnowCat cabin seats 19, with the windows providing a full 360-degree panoramic view. The going is slow, letting you soak up the spirit of a night on Blackcomb Mountain. My group included a family of eight from Mexico, two US doctors, a Vancouver filmmaker, a former South American beauty queen, and others. We got to know one another over a fondue dinner in the Crystal Hut. But the best part, the part I can't forget, was going outside, away from the lights, and looking up. From the top of the mountain the view of the star-filled night sky was thrilling, with the stars appearing so close I felt I could touch them.

SNOWMOBILING AND SNOWCAT

The snowmobiles don't loiter after an evening fondue at the Crystal Hut at 1,828m (6,000 ft.). The drivers zoom down Blackcomb Mountain to complete the 4-hour dinner ride with **Canadian Snowmobile Adventures** (© **604/938-1616,** www.cdn-snowmobile. com). For a single it's C$199 (US$125), and C$159 (US$99.35) for sharing a snowmobile. Another tour takes in the Callaghan Wilderness, the site of the 2010 Whistler Winter Olympic bid. **Blackcomb Snowmobile** (© **604/932-8484,** www.snowmobiling.bc.ca) has a

4-hour early bird Blackcomb Mountain tour. Start at 8am with Whistler's best breakfast at Chef Bernard's, then head for high alpine powder at elevations of 1,981m (6,499 ft.). The cost is C$229 (US$143) for a single, and C$169 (US$105.60) per person. **Cougar Mountain** is a good choice (© **604/932-5046,** www.cougar mountain.ca) to experience the backcountry close to Whistler. The Ancient Cedars tour visits a 1,000-year-old grove, with a stop at the rustic Trapper's Cabin for a hearty Canadian lunch. Prices range from C$99 to C$169 (US$61.85 to US$105.60).

SNOWSHOEING

Snowshoeing is a classic Canadian activity that's really caught on in the past few years. It's inexpensive and suited to a wide range of people. While it does take some physical effort, it's easy to learn and you can wear your own shoes if they're warm and waterproof. Snowshoes can be rented at a number of places in Whistler, or bring your own. Dedicated trails wind through the forests of Lost Lake Park, and you can use them for a trail fee of C$10 (US$6.25). Keep to the marked trails and refrain from snowshoeing on groomed ski trails. Snowshoe by snowmobile with **Canadian Snowmobile Adventures** (© **877/938-1616,** 604/938-1616, www.cdn-snowmobile.com). Journey to the beautiful Fitzsimmons Creek log bridge, strap on your snowshoes, and follow your guide on a fun and leisurely trek along the Hidden Valley between Whistler and Blackcomb mountains. Cost is C$109 (US$68) for a single rider, C$79 (US$49.35) for two sharing the 2.5-hour tour. Departs daily at 9am. Kids 12 and under free with each full-fare adult. **Cougar Mountain at Whistler** (© **888/297-2222,** 604/ 932-4086, www.cougarmountain.ca) has guided tours to the back-country for some 20 years. Whether you're a first-timer or a sea-soned veteran, the introductory Backcountry Nature Tour provides a wonderful memory of the Cougar Mountain Wilderness area. The 2-hour tour departs at 10:30am, noon, and 3pm. Cost is C$49 (US$30.60), and for children 12 and under with an adult it's half-price. Another fascinating snowshoeing expedition is the Parkhurst Ghost Town Hike with **Whistler Outdoor Experience** (© **877/386-1888,** 604/932-3389, www.whistleroutdoor.com). The 3-hour hike, at C$65 (US$40.60) for adults and C$21.50 (US$13.45) for children under 12, includes equipment, beverages, and energy snacks. They can also set you up on a self-guided tour with rental equipment and a map so that you can visit Parkhurst on your own.

7 Rental Shops

Rental shops are at various locations, so call for the one nearest you. You can rent high-performance and regular skis, snowboards, telemark and cross-country skis, and snowshoes from many of these companies.

Affinity Sports ✆ **604/932-6611,** 604/932-6461

Breeze Ski Rental ✆ **604/938-7749** Blackcomb Daylodge, ✆ **604/938-7749** Carleton Lodge

Escape Route Adventure Group ✆ **604/938-3228,** fax 604/938-9066

Katmandu Mountain Sports ✆ and fax **604/932-6381**

Spicy Sports ✆ **604/932-6225** or 604/938-6225, fax 604/938-4900

Sportstop ✆ **604/932-5495,** fax 604/932-2578

Summit Ski ✆ **604/932-6225** or 604/938-6225, fax 604/932-2057

Whistler Village Sports ✆ **604/932-2578**

Wild Willies Ski Club ✆ **604/938-8836,** fax 604/938-1979

Whistler/Blackcomb rental shops:

Blackcomb Base II Rentals ✆ **604/938-7228**

Carleton Rentals ✆ **604/905-2250**

Creekside Rentals ✆ **604/905-2141**

Essentially Blackcomb Hi Pro ✆ **604/938-7777**

Gondola Rentals ✆ **604/905-2252**

Mountain Adventure Centre ✆ **604/938-7737** (Blackcomb Daylodge), ✆ **604/938-7737** (Pan Pacific Lodge), ✆ **604/938-2017** (Fairmont Chateau Whistler)

Mountain Adventure Centre II ✆ **604/905-3653**

On-Line Rentals ✆ **604/938-7518**

Rossignol Store ✆ **604/905-3653**

Showcase Rentals ✆ **604/905-2246**

Salomon@Whistler ✆ **604/905-2262**

Sportswest Rentals ✆ **604/905-2250**

Trax & Trails ✆ **604/938-2017**

Village Rentals ✆ **604/905-2252**

West Coast Rentals ✆ **604/938-7749**

Kids Kamp Rental ✆ **604/938-7310**

8 Special Winter Events

AltitudeX   Now attracting more than 2,500 gay and lesbian visitors, AltitudeX ski week was launched in 1993 with 200 local gay and lesbian skiers. It now hosts some 30 different events and activities during the first week of February, and attracts many international visitors. Events start in Vancouver, then move on to Whistler. Both mountains and just about every venue and hotel in the resort get involved. A full-week pass is C$525 (US$328) for all ticketed AltitudeX events, plus goodies such as an AltitudeX T-shirt. A half-week pass is C$315 (US$196). Individual tickets to various events are also available. The best advice is to buy your tickets very early, as many events (such as the beach party at Meadow Park Sports Centre) sell out almost instantly. ℭ **888/258-4883,** 604/899-6209, fax 604/899-6214, www.outontheslopes.com.

First Night Whistler—A Family Celebration of the Arts (ℭ **604/932-5535**)   Leave your bottle at home on New Year's Eve if you head for Whistler Village. The Resort Municipality of Whistler's First Night is a liquor-free event, and more than 100 police officers are on duty to keep it that way. This family-oriented participatory arts festival showcases music, street performers, and arts and crafts workshops throughout the resort. The event kicks off with a People's Procession from the Whistler Conference Centre in Whistler Village to the Town Plaza in Village North, featuring larger-than-life puppets and banners. Dress up, bring your drums, horns, and noisemakers, and join the walk. More than a dozen street entertainment acts include fire jugglers, blues musicians, children's entertainment, and roving comedy. Individual tickets are C$15 (US$9.35); the family package is C$30 (US$18.75). Bus service is free.

Ski and Snowboard Competitions   Every month sees a number of competitions. In early December, for example, **Nokia Snowboard FIS World Cup** lures the best riders in the world to compete for C$160,000 (US$100,000), the largest single-stop cash prize purse of the World Cup circuit in North America. Competitions include parallel giant slalom racing, freestyle halfpipe, and snowboard-cross events. Halfpipe competitors are judged on a combo of height for each hit, rotations, technical difficulty, and smoothness of landings. Snowboard cross sees riders racing four at a time through a course of banked turns, jumps, and mogul fields. In late January, the annual **FIS World Cup Freestyle Skiing** competition showcases the world's best freestyle skiers in both aerial and mogul competitions on

Blackcomb Mountain. Some 200 athletes and officials from over 20 countries take part. March hosts the **Couloir Extreme Race International,** where extreme skiers compete on Blackcomb Mountain. In April, **Whistler Cup** sees the world's best juvenile racers in competition. The **Mouton Cadet Spring Festival** on Whistler Mountain also hosts 2 days of individual and team ski races, including a costume competition, followed by an on-mountain picnic and barbecue each day. **The World Ski & Snowboard Festival** (www.wssf.com), a 10-day event in mid-April, is North America's largest winter sports and music festival. The non-stop action includes free outdoor concerts every day in Whistler Village, world-class ski and snowboard competitions, demo days, and much more. Party hearty is the motto of this event, with thousands of revelers dancing in the Village streets. For more information on the above events, call Ⓒ **800/766-0449,** 604/932-3434, www.whistler-blackcomb.com.

6

Summer Pursuits

What goes around, comes around. In 1914 Alex and Myrtle Philip opened Rainbow Lodge on Alta Lake, and soon had visitors hiking in with packhorses to fish and enjoy the mountain air. The lodge burned down in 1978, and by the late 1980s Whistler was recognized as a premier ski resort. Over the past 10 years, though, Whistler has regained its reputation as a summer resort, now attracting almost as many visitors between June and mid-September as it does in winter. The long summer days are not blisteringly hot, with an average temperature of 21°C (71°F), but hot enough to swim, hike, or bike in comfort. Although the resort tends to buzz with visitors, it's still more laidback, which is very appealing to some.

The mountains and the resort's five lakes are still here. What has changed is the new ways you can experience them, from in-line skating to helicopter flights. Mountain biking is now hugely popular. Then there's golf, the summer passion for many, with three designer courses in Whistler, plus two in Pemberton 25 minutes north. (For mountain biking and golf, see below.)

Whistler is promoted as a four-season destination, although in spring and fall you'll find some attractions closed. On the other hand, many visitors prefer the significantly lower off-season prices, ample parking, and the quieter ambience of the hotels, restaurants, and cafes in the spring and fall.

As summer grows in popularity, it's important to plan your trip and book ahead for accommodations and camping. You might even get a good package that will save you money.

Plan and book your activities through **Tourism Whistler,** the resort's official reservation service (4010 Whistler Way, Whistler, BC V0N 1B4, ℂ **800/944-7853,** 604/932-2394, www.tourismwhistler.com). Or visit the Whistler Activity and Information Centre in the Whistler Conference Centre, Whistler Village, also run by Tourism Whistler.

For anything to do with Whistler and Blackcomb mountain summer activities, you can also contact **Whistler/Blackcomb Mountain** (4545 Blackcomb Way, Whistler, BC V0N IB4, ℂ **800/766-0449,**

604/932-3434, www.whistlerblackcomb.com). The website is a good way to get to know what's happening on the mountains.

You can also call **individual activity providers** at the numbers noted in "Other Activities" later in this chapter.

Summer spreads out the activities. Visitors flock to Whistler and Blackcomb mountains to mountain bike, ski, hike, and sightsee, but they also spend more time elsewhere. Driving is easy and the nights are long, so spend some time exploring. Head north to Pemberton, or even farther north to Birkenhead Provincial Park (see chapter 10, "Side Trips"). It's an easy day's drive, and you can take a picnic or buy food along the way.

When you need a break from all that healthy physical stuff, take in some culture. Street entertainers, band concerts, art shows, jazz, blues, and even symphony concerts will entertain you and your family. Annual festivals add energy, including the World Beat Music Weekend in June, the Celebration of Aboriginal Culture in August, and Oktoberfest in October (see chapter 1, "Planning a Trip to Whistler," for summer festival listings). If you're serious about art, and curious about how local artists live, you can also arrange studio visits (see "Studio Visits" later in this chapter).

Summer is a great season for children. They can bike and swim at the lakes, take tennis lessons, in-line skate, hike together as a family, ride horses, see first-run movies at Rainbow Theatre (*©* **604/932-2422**), and much more.

1 The Mountains in Summer

Whistler and Blackcomb mountains don't give up on fun in the summer.

BLACKCOMB MOUNTAIN
BLACKCOMB BASE ADVENTURE ZONE   For thrill-seekers of all ages, the adventure zone offers a huge variety of activities for the entire family. An 18-hole mini-golf course, the Great Wall Climbing Centre, horseback and all-terrain vehicle tours, Kiss the Sky trampoline, and the brand new Luge (an exhilarating 1.4km [.86 mile] cart luge track), are all just a short walk from Whistler Village at the base of Blackcomb Mountain.

GLACIER SKIING AND SNOWBOARDING   Blackcomb's **Horstman Glacier** is one of Canada's only places for summer skiing and snowboarding. The glacier covers 112 acres of terrain and is located at an elevation of 2,330m (7,642 ft.).

Daily skiing and snowboarding starts in mid-June and runs to the end of the first week of August, from noon to 3pm, with public access from 11am. You'll find yourself alongside some of North America's finest athletes training for upcoming competitions. The glacier terrain is suitable for intermediate to advanced skiers and riders.

Camps include **Smart Mogul Skiing** with John Smart (© **604/905-4421,** www.smartmogul.com), **High North** new school skiing camp with Shane Szocs and JP Auclair (www.highnorth skicamp.com), and **Dave Murray Summer Ski and Snowboard Camp** (© **604/932-5765,** www.skiandsnowboard.com). The biggest of all is the legendary **Camp of Champions Summer Snowboard Camp** (© **888/997-2267,** www.campofchampions. com), with top North American coaches. Mornings are spent on the glacier, afternoons in the valley skateboarding, mountain biking, or hanging out at Whistler's lakes. This is a great program for kids 11 and up.

WHISTLER MOUNTAIN
SIGHTSEEING No summer visit is complete without a trip to the top of Whistler Mountain. The Whistler Village gondola runs from the end of June to the third week in September, and on weekends only from late September to the end of the first week in October. Times are 10am to 5pm, Sunday to Friday; and 10am to 8pm on Saturdays only. The gondola ride is in a class of its own: it has full valley views and will take you to the top in 20 minutes. On the way up, look for wildlife grazing on the ski runs, especially black bears. At the top you'll find more than 48km (30 miles) of hiking trails, ranging from gentle paths awash in alpine wildflowers to rough-hewn fields of granite. Refreshments are available at Roundhouse Lodge. Take a free guided hiking tour or hire a personal guide for your group. Tours depart daily from Roundhouse Lodge at 11am and 1:30pm. Tours meet at the light board, weather permitting.

There is no summer sightseeing on Blackcomb Mountain at this time, although this is under consideration.

Hiking Trails on Whistler Mountain Nine hiking trails range from somewhat difficult to difficult. **Paleface Trail** is a somewhat challenging 1km (.6 mile) hike to view extinct volcanoes, with an elevation gain of 85m (279 ft.). **Ridge Lookout** is a 1.2km (.7 mile) short, steep hike offering a spectacular view. **Glacier Trail** takes approximately 60 minutes return to cover a distance of 2.5km (1.55 miles), and offers views of Whistler Glacier.

Three more challenging hikes are **Harmony Meadows,** with views of Fitzsimmons Valley and Harmony Lakes, 2.6km (1.6 miles), and **Harmony Lake Trail & Loop,** 2km (1.25 miles) to Harmony Lake or 3.5km (2.2 miles) including Harmony Loop. **Village Descent** features valley viewpoints and forested sections for 10km (6.2 miles) one way only.

Three difficult trails are for the very physically fit. **Musical Bumps to Singing Pass** in Garibaldi Provincial Park is a 5- to 6-hour hike of 19km (11.8 miles) one way to Whistler Village. En route you'll see views of Black Tusk, Cheakamus Glacier, and Cheakamus Lake. **Burnt Stew** is only 20 minutes in length but has an elevation gain of 100m (1.3 miles) covering 2.2km (1.3 miles). This will also connect you to Musical Bumps. The reward is views of Fitzsimmons Valley. Also difficult is **Little Whistler Trail,** a 3.8km (2 mile) hike with a 265m (870 ft.) elevation gain to an impressive view of Black Tusk.

(Fun Fact **Where Does the Name "Whistler" Come From?**

Whistler was named for the bug-eyed, beaver-toothed hoary marmot. The critter, which looks something like a big ground-hog, makes a distinctive whistling sound when signaling danger. "Hoary" refers to the animal's fur, which is brown with grey tips, as if it's been frosted. Look for marmots sunning themselves on rocks if you're hiking on top of Whistler Mountain.

TICKETS FOR SUMMER MOUNTAIN ACTIVITIES
Whistler Mountain is open daily for sightseeing and mountain biking from late June to the third week of September. Tickets are required, and can be purchased at the Whistler Village Gondola. Whistler Mountain sightseeing costs C$22 (US$13.75) for adults, C$19 (US$11.85) for youth/seniors, and C$5 (US$3.10) for children 7 to 12. Free for those 6 and under. A summer sightseeing pass is C$33 (US$20.60) and allows unlimited access.

A 1-day **Whistler Mountain Bike Park** ticket is C$32 (US$20) for adults and $C29 (US$18.10) for youth 13 to 18. A bike-park season pass is C$199 (US$124.35) for adults and youth. A pass-holder day rate of C$10 for adults and youth applies to individuals who already have a sightseeing lift ticket. A combined sightseeing and bike park pass is C$158 (US$98.75). The park is not recommended for children under 12.

A **Blackcomb Mountain** glacier skiing/snowboarding ticket is C$39 (US$24.35) for adults and C$32 (US$20) for youth/seniors.

(Tips) **Hiking Safety**

You see them all the time at the top of the Whistler Village Gondola, shivering in the mountain breeze or sunburned from overexposure to the strong rays of the sun. Hiking on the mountain is one of the must-do summer activities, but it does require common sense. Never hike alone in a mountain environment. Weather changes are common, so bring extra warm clothing. Stay on marked trails to avoid damage to the alpine ecosystem. Observe all closures. Steep slopes, snow, and ice fields are very dangerous. Treat all wildlife with caution. Do not feed or approach bears. Carry a watch and make note of the last lift down. Carry water, a snack, sunscreen, and bug spray. If you encounter explosives (left over from winter avalanche control) stay 3m (6.5 ft.) away and call mountain staff. Do not touch.

---

2 Wild & Crazy Mountain Biking

Whistler is now one of the world's leading mountain bike resort destinations. In addition to Whistler Mountain, which definitely has the terrain for the sport, there are hundreds of kilometers of trails through mountainous terrain along the Sea to Sky corridor. On a Saturday morning, some 200 people and bikes will be waiting for the Whistler Village Gondola to head up to the top of Whistler Mountain. Last summer the mountain's Bike Park averaged 300 people a day, and that's only a small percentage of all the riders in Whistler Valley. Buy a bike map, available at many retail outlets, and get rolling.

BIKING ON WHISTLER MOUNTAIN   To bike on the mountain, take the Whistler Mountain Gondola to groomed trails, self-guided areas, tours, professional instructors, three trial parks, and miles of single-track trail. The descent from the top is more than 1,968m (6,000 ft.). Due to the size of the mountain, full descents are available only with a guide. You'll be put into a group with others who match your ability and stamina. Adult half-day descent with a guide, lift ticket, and bike rental is C$95 (US$60) for adults and C$75 (US$46.85) for youth. For a full day it's C$115 (US$71.85) for adults and C$95 (US$60) for youth. You can ride all trails from Olympic Station without a guide.

Guides and instructors are certified through the Canadian National Coaching Certification Program. Private lessons are available. Those with less time can join a guided cross-country tour from the base of Whistler Mountain. For 2 hours, ride with a guide beside local rivers, visit hidden lakes, and take in mountain views. Tour and bike rental is C$55 (US$21.85) for adults and C$35 (US$21.85) for youth.

Whistler Mountain Bike Park   The newly developed Whistler Mountain Bike Park offers terrain for everyone, from families looking for guided descents to the hardcore downhiller. The lift-accessed park has over 20 trails and three trails parks. Green, blue, and double-black skills centers are designed for different levels of ability.

The park is a short ride up the Whistler Village Gondola to 1,019m (3,343 ft.). Descent is by way of multiple routes down old trails and ski runs, leading riders of all levels to the valley floor.

Bike Programs   Riding programs run May through September. For more information on all programs noted below, contact ✆ **800/ 766-0449,** 604/932-3434 to register and receive an info package by mail, or go to **www.whistlerblackcomb.com.**

A great women's program is the **Spokeswomen Mountain Bike Camps,** where you can learn everything from bike fit and maintenance to off-road single-track skills. Programs for more advanced women riders are also offered. Adult 2-day weekend camps start Friday night and continue to Sunday. The camp and lift ticket is C$299 (US$186.85); with bike, add C$35 (US$21.85). You can also learn with **Richey Schley Freeride Camps** for intermediate to advanced riders of all ages, and with **Summer Gravity Camps,** weeklong summer camps for youth aged 13 to 18. Schley is well-known as the 1993 Canadian BMX champion, the star of the *Kranked Series* videos, and a freeriding pioneer. Two-day weekend camps run from the end of May to late August at a cost of C$299 (US$186.85); add C$80 (US$50) for bike rental. Daily Learn to Ride clinics provide the basics while freeride clinics provide mastery of drop-off, elevated trails, planks, ladders, and big air.

BIKE RENTALS AND MORE   Rent from two Whistler/Black-comb **Glacier Shop** locations (at the base of the Whistler Village Gondola and in the Upper Village across from the Fairmont Chateau Whistler). Take out a bike for 1 to 3 hours, or for a full day. All rental bikes are full-suspension hi-pro styles and include helmet rental (required by law in British Columbia). Package rates including rental, helmet, gloves, and bike lock are available. Bikes rent for an average of C$10 (US$6.25) per hour. Full day and package rates give you something of a price break.

Several dozen more **local bike shops** rent everything from a tot's bike to body armor for the bush rider. Drop in to check out what's new. Expert mechanics can repair your own bike in a day. Eric Wight is owner of one of the oldest shops, **Backroads Bikes & Boats** (© 604/932-3111, www.whistlermountainbiking.com), established in 1985. Wight was one of the early designers of Whistler Mountain's Bike Park back in 1995, in the days when dual-suspension bikes were something new. Now you're likely to see riders in full armor and face helmets on bikes valued at many thousands of dollars. Ask about private guided mountain biking, just you and your friends for C$70 (US$43.75), a fixed price for up to four people for a 2-hour tour.

Many of the province's leading manufacturers of bikes, components, and riding wear have shops in Whistler. **Race Face** supplies cranks, rings, and headsets to professional racers, and shops are well-stocked with these strong and colorful parts. **Rocky Mountain** and **Brodie** bicycles are made-in-BC full-suspension bikes available for rent. The technician fitting you may be a former racing champion, so don't be shy about asking about past achievements. Local tips and riding hints could prevent an accident. If you're a slower-paced rider, try a cruiser bike with curvy, fat tires. **Roach** (so named because "you can't kill a roach") body armor and clothing, developed by a Vancouver woman, has indestructible shorts that your kids will love for their cool style. Another line of shorts, jerseys, and long pants, also quite indestructible, are made by **Hoots.**

3 Golf: The Summer Passion

Golf in the Whistler area is now so good that *Golf Digest* proclaimed Whistler the number one golf destination in Canada (and number 19 in the world) in 2000. With three designer golf courses in Whistler and two in nearby Pemberton (plus two in Squamish and one in Furry Creek—see chapter 10, "Side Trips"), you can golf a new course every day of the week. Adding to the choice (and also adding to the prices) are the absolutely gorgeous settings enjoyed by these courses .

Rates are based on the 2001 golf season and are subject to change. Whistler-area courses are open for the season between mid-April and May 1.

WHISTLER COURSES

The Chateau Whistler Golf Club   Awarded a Gold Medal by the New York–based *Golf Magazine,* the club is conveniently located at the base of Blackcomb Mountain (© **877/938-2092,** 604/938-2092, www.chateauwhistlergolf.com). This is an 18-hole, par-72 course with an elevation gain of more than 92m (300 ft.), a superb test of golf. Designed by Robert Trent Jones Jr., it opened in 1993. In 2001 it was awarded *Condé Nast Traveler's* Best Golf Resort in North America, Mexico, and the Caribbean. Terraces overlook Whistler Village and Green Lake; at the third tee, you look straight up at a wall of towering Douglas firs along the right side of the fairway that continues up to the mountain peaks. The course traverses mountain ledges and crosses cascading creeks. Mid-course, you get a panoramic view of the Coast Mountains. Add to this the splendid Fairmont Chateau Whistler patio for après-golf relaxing, and you have all-round golf heaven. Peak-season greens fees are C$205 daily (US$128) and C$130 (US$81.25) at twilight (includes golf-cart rental).

Nicklaus North Golf Course   A multiple-award-winning 18-hole golf course 2km (1.24 miles) north of Whistler Village (© **800/386-9898,** 604/938-9898, www.nicklausnorth.com). The setting on the shores of Green Lake, with 360-degree views of Whistler/Blackcomb mountains, Wedge and Rainbow mountains, and Armchair Glacier, is amazingly beautiful. Opened in 1996, the par-71 course is one of only two Canadian courses designed by Jack Nicklaus. Jack visited Whistler six times during construction, and this is the only course worldwide that carries his name. Peak-season greens fees are C$125 to C$205 (US$78.10 to US$128.10) and C$125 (US$78) at twilight, and include a GPS-equipped power cart and full use of the practice facility with a 274m (300 yd.) driving range. Notable features include bent-grass tees, practice sand traps, and a 280 sq. m (3,000 sq. ft.) putting and chipping green. When it opened, it was named Best New Canadian Golf Course by *Golf*

Digest magazine. It's designed with resort play in mind, with five par-3s shaped to command the players' attention, especially the 17th signature hole at 206m (226 yd.), arguably one of the most spectacular par 3s anywhere in the world. **Joel's Restaurant at Nicklaus North** (© 604/932-1240) is open for breakfast and snacks, and lunch all afternoon with fondues, fresh seafood, pastas, and BBQs. The patio dining makes the most of the view.

Whistler Golf Course   Designed by Arnold Palmer, the course features nine lakes, two winding creeks, rolling greens, and magnificent vistas (© **800/376-1777,** 604/932-4544, www.whistler golf.com). In 2000 it underwent a C$2-million (US$1.25-million) renovation. The 18-hole, par-72 course offers a driving range, putting green, sand bunker, and pitching area. The picturesque setting is very appealing. Although not overly long, the course benefits from southerly afternoon winds that make it play much longer. Greens fees are variable, depending on the season and the time of day. Summer season (July 4 to Sept 8) rates range from C$159 (US$99.35) for the day to C$99 (US$61.85) at twilight.

PEMBERTON COURSES

Pemberton is hotter and sunnier than Whistler, and only a half-hour drive north.

Big Sky Golf & Country Club   This club is located in one of the most beautiful mountain valleys in the world (© **800/668-7900,** 604/894-6106, www.bigskygolf.com). The 18-hole championship course was designed by award-winning Bob Cupp. In 2000 it was ranked the number one course for women golfers, and facility of the year in 1998. Includes a fine-dining restaurant. The summer rate from Monday to Friday is C$135 (US$84.35), on weekends/holidays it's C$150 (US$93.75). If you arrive before 7am, or late afternoon to twilight, rates are lower. The Big Sky Golf Academy was cited by *Golf Ranking Magazine Canada* as a top-ranked golf academy, with practice and teaching facility for tees, greens, sand traps, water hazards, practice holes, and a variety of shot-making opportunities. Instructions are available for every age and skill level.

Pemberton Valley Golf & Country Club   Opened in 1989, the course is 18 holes, par 72 (© **800/390-4653,** 604/894-6197, www. pembertongolf.com). Excellent bent-grass greens and an island golf green. The website has an outstanding virtual tour. For value for money, this can't be beat, offering top-quality golf at a more affordable price. The low-season, mid-week rate is C$50 (US$31.25); the high-season mid-week rate is C$58 (US$36.25). In high season, the rate from Friday to Sunday, including holidays, is C$70 (US$43.75).

Value Tee-time Hotline

Last Minute Golf Hotline (© 800/684-6344, 604/878-1833) will save you time and money. Call to arrange a next-day tee time at Whistler golf courses and at over 30 courses elsewhere in BC. Savings can be as much as 40% on next-day, last-minute tee times. No membership is necessary. Call between 3pm and 9pm for the next day or before noon for the same day. The hotline also arranges advanced bookings as much as a year ahead, as well as group bookings.

---

4 Other Summer Pursuits

ALL TERRAIN VEHICLES (ATV)

All terrain vehicles may at first seem out of place in the scenic beauty of Whistler, but companies follow strict guidelines to protect the environment. Riding today's quieter, modern ATVs gets you to remote areas that are otherwise difficult to reach. Tours vary in price, starting at around C$89 (US$55.60), with passengers paying a reduced rate. On Blackcomb Mountain, **Canadian All Terrain Adventures** (© 877/938-1616, 604/938-1616, www.cdn-snow mobile.com) offers a beginner trips such as a ride to Whistler's hidden valley with views of the dual mountains and pristine Fitz-simmons watershed. If you want to ford streams, blast a mud bog, and ride up and over sand piles and logs, ask for the Crazy Horse tour. **Cougar Mountain at Whistler** (© 888/297-2222, 604/932-4086, cougarmountain.ca) explores the backcountry north of Whistler. Tours include the 2-hour Bear Paw beginner trip through country that is home to moose, deer, and other wildlife, and the ATV/hike combo to the Ancient Cedars, a protected grove of 1,000-year-old Red Cedar trees perched on the West Slope of Cougar Mountain. **Outdoor Adventures@Whistler** (© 604/932-0647, www.adventures whistler.com) explores scenic trails in the nearby Soo Valley and lookouts on Rainbow Mountain.

Whistler in Summer

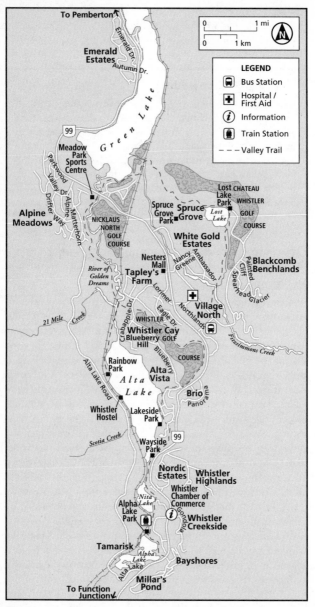

To Pemberton

Emerald Estates

Emerald Dr.

Autumn Dr.

0   1 mi
0   1 km

N

LEGEND
- 🚍 Bus Station
- ➕ Hospital / First Aid
- ⓘ Information
- 🏠 Train Station
- – – – Valley Trail

Green Lake

99

Meadow Park Sports Centre

Parkwood

Valley Dr.

Matterhorn

Drifter Way

Alpine

Alpine Meadows

NICKLAUS NORTH GOLF COURSE

River of Golden Dreams

21 Mile Creek

Spruce Grove Park

Spruce Grove

Lost Lake Park

Lost Lake

CHATEAU WHISTLER GOLF COURSE

White Gold Estates

Nancy Greene

Ambassador

Blackcomb Benchlands

Cliff

Painted

Spearhead Glacier

Nesters Mall

Tapley's Farm

Lorimer

Eagle Dr.

Crabapple Dr.

WHISTLER

Whistler Cay

Blueberry Hill

Blueberry

GOLF COURSE

Northlands

Village North

Fitzsimmons Creek

Rainbow Park

Alta Lake

Alta Vista

Brio

Panorama

Whistler Hostel

Lakeside Park

Alta Lake Road

Scotia Creek

Wayside Park

99

Nordic Estates

Whistler Highlands

Whistler Chamber of Commerce

Nita Lake

Alpha Lake Park

ⓘ

Gondola

Whistler Creekside

Tamarisk

Alpha Lake

Bayshores

Alta

To Function Junction

Millar's Pond

Fun Fact   **How High Is Whistler?**

Whistler's base elevation is 675m (2,214 ft.) and its peak elevation is 2,284m (7,494 ft.).

WATER SPORTS

Whistler has to be the luckiest resort, with mountains, valleys, lakes, and rivers in abundance. Water sports are fun and well-regulated for safety. One of the oldest companies is **Whistler Backroads Adventure Tours** (© 604/932-3111, www.whistlermountain biking.com). Recall the days of pioneers Alex and Myrtle Philip with a canoe or kayak tour on the River of Golden Dreams. This trip was a favorite of Alex's, inspiring him to write bad poetry. After a short drive to Alta Lake and a quick canoe lesson, you'll be heading for Lilypad Flat to practice your newfound skills. Then it's up the river, a flat but twisty route through wetlands with ducks, beaver, and mink. In the fall, water levels permitting, you may be able to paddle to the ghost town of Parkhurst, an abandoned logging camp. Long-gone Mrs. Valleau's garden is still tended by local women who canoe across the lake daily. Tours are C$62.50 (US$39) guided, $35 (US$21.85) unguided. **Whistler Outdoor Experience** (© 877/386-1888, 604/932-3389, www.whistleroutdoor.com) offers canoe-ing, kayaking, sailing, windsurfing, pedal boats, and fishing boats on Green and Alta lakes. The 2-hour Alta to Green Lake canoe ride on the River of Golden Dreams is a Class 1 paddle (mighty mellow) at C$60 per person (US$37.50) guided; unguided C$35 (US$21.85), kids 12 and under half-price. **Wedge Rafting** (© 888/932-5899, 604/932-7171, www.wedgerafting.com) has whitewater tours suit-able for first-timers as well as more experienced rafters. The Green River tour, at C$64 (US$40), is paddle rafting for healthy, active people. For more challenging whitewater, try the Birkenhead tour, May to June, around the scenic Pemberton Valley with an 8km (5 mile) river run. The cost is C$82 (US$51.25). Children 16 and under are C$10 (US$6.25) off any tour. **Whistler River Adventures** (© 888/932-3532, 604/932-3532, www.whistlerriver.com) offer tours that range from 2-hour to full-day fully guided rafting runs. The half-day Birkenhead River tour is very popular, suiting up at **The Adventure Ranch** for the trip through old-growth forests, with continuous whitewater action thrills for the entire family. The cost is C$82 (US$51.25) per adult, C$72 (US$45) for children 16 and under. All tours meet in Whistler Village. Children and youths must weigh at least 90 pounds.

Finds **The Adventure Ranch**

True, it's north of Whistler, almost in Pemberton, but **The Adventure Ranch** (© 604/894-5200, www.whistlerriver.com) is worth the 35-minute drive. The 10-acre ranch at the foot of 2,438-m (8,000 ft.) Mt. Currie is such a pleasant place to spend the day. You can horseback ride, jetboat on the Lillooet River that flows by the property, or take a haywagon tour. Or you can do just about nothing. Lounge by the swimming pool on the large covered deck, or play lawn sports. Order up a cappuccino before the daily lunch special, which features Texas BBQs, deli sandwiches, and home-baked breads. At night, cuddle before a bonfire with the stars twinkling over-head before returning to Whistler. The Adventure Shop sells crafts, souvenirs, snacks, and drinks.

FISHING

With its remote alpine lakes and crystal clear mountain rivers, the Whistler area boasts spring runs of steelhead, rainbow trout, cut-throat trout, and Dolly Varden char. In summer, there are runs of cutthroat and salmon, and in the fall, runs of Coho salmon in the glacier-fed lakes and rivers. You'll need a fishing license, which costs around C$15 (US$9.35) a day, purchased from the activity providers noted here. **Whistler Fishing Guides** (© 604/932-4267, www.whistlerriver.com) feature guided fishing experiences in the Sea to Sky corridor between Squamish and Lillooet depending on the season, with fly, spin, and drift fishing instructions, and include equipment and tackle. Rates are from C$150 to C$295 (US$93.75 to US$184). **Cougar Mountain at Whistler** (© 888/932-9998, 604/932-4086, www.cougarmountain.ca) offers year-round fishing trips plus a full-service store in Village North at 36-4314 Main St. Stop by for a daily report on the local fishing hot spots and what to use. All trips are strictly catch-and-release for the purpose of preserving a quality angling experience. A 2-hour learn-to-fly-fish-with-professionals lesson is C$39 (US$24.35) per person. Private lessons are C$39 (US$24.35) per hour. Lessons include equipment. **Whistler Flyfishing** is one-stop shopping, including a guide service, flyfishing school, and fly shop at 126-4340 Lorimer Rd. in Whistler Marketplace (*©* **888/822-3474 US only,** 604/932-7221, www. whistlerflyfishing.com). Their summer-only store is open from May 1 to the end of September. Whistler Flyfishing specializes in private casting lessons, guided trips, and overnight trips. They have certified flyfishing and flycasting teachers, and provide high-quality flyfishing equipment as well as transportation to and from your Whistler accommodation. A lunch is included in the full-day excursions. The half-day rate is C$205 (US$128.10); a group of two or more is C$140 (US87.50) per person. The full-day (9-hr. minimum) rate is C$295 (US$184.35) for one person; for two or more it's C$185 (US$115.60) per person. Overnight trips and single-day float trips, fly outs, and heli-fishing can also be arranged. The half-day excursion to the Upper Cheakamus River is convenient and very popular. If you're feeling extravagant, fly off Green Lake in a Beaver airplane to Campbell River on the west coast. Board a 26-foot jet boat, then fish remote Bute Inlet. Cost is approximately C$4,000 (US$2,500) for a group of four.

HELICOPTER TOURS

The optimal season for flightseeing is summer. **Blackcomb Helicopters** (*©* **800/330-4354,** 604/938-1700, www.blackcomb helicopters.com) lets you see Whistler the way the eagles see it, with flightseeing tours, glacier landings, heli-fishing, heli-biking, heli-ski programs, heli-snowmobiling, and heli-wedding packages. Year-round and summer tours range from C$149 to C$319 (US$93 to US$199) for 20- to 45-minute flights. The Mountain Top Heli Tour departs from the top of Whistler Mountain (valid lift ticket required) for 8- and 12-minute flights at C$59 to C$89 (US$38.85 to US$55.60). The company is based at the Whistler Municipal Heliport, 10km (6.25 miles) north of the Village. For nearly 20 years, **Whistler Air Services** (*©* **888/806-2299,** 604/932-6615, www.whisair.com) pilots have provided colorful commentary via stereo headsets to their passengers. To land on a glacial lake, take the 70-minute Lake Lovelywater Tour at C$159 (US$100). The 30-minute Glacier Tour is C$99 (US$61.85) for an eagle's eye view of Garibaldi Provincial Park's immense glaciers, volcanic craters, and deep blue alpine lakes. The 40-minute Ice Cap Tour is C$129 (US$80.60). Whistler Air is located on the south shore of Green Lake north of Whistler Village.

> *Fun Fact* **Weddings Are Big Business**
>
> Destination weddings, which include the destination as part of the occasion for family and friends, are year-round big business in Whistler. International visitors make up 80% of Whistler Wedding Planners clientele (② **604/932-4672,** www.whistlerweddingplanners.com). Owner Linda Marshall's couples come from England, the Pacific Northwest (because of the American dollar), Canada, and elsewhere. Favorite spots to tie the knot include Whistler Mountain top, Lost Lake, and historic locales such as Rainbow Park on Alta Lake. Fairmont Chateau Whistler's Woodlands Terrace is also very popular. Some get married in ski suits, others in beautiful gowns. The most spectacular are heli-weddings, with 20-minute fly-ins by **Blackcomb Helicopters** (② **800/330-4354,** ② **604/938-1700,** www.black combhelicopters.com) to the top of Mt. Currie or Table Mountain. Linda once shoveled a heart in the snow to let the pilot know where she was waiting with the champagne and flowers.

HIKING & SIGHTSEEING

Hiking is one of the best ways to connect to the area's many natural beauties. In addition to hiking and sightseeing on Whistler Mountain (see above), there are hundreds of other easy to challenging trails. Get to know the area with a guided tour, or buy a trail map from a local retail shop and explore away.

GUIDED TOURS　Join a hiking tour or hire a personal guide for your group. For a freebie (once you're on the Whistler Mountain), head for the light board at The Roundhouse, daily at 11am and 1:30pm, weather permitting. Farther afield, you have a wealth of choices with a dozen different companies. Nature Walks for Seniors are led by **Backroads Bikes & Boats** (② **604/932-3111,** www.whistlermountainbiking.com). The 2-hour easy walks take you to Lost Lake Park or to BC provincial parks to visit Cheakamus Lake or Brandywine Falls south of Whistler, C$49 (US$30.60). Private nature walk trips for the family (four people) can be arranged for C$250 (US$156.25). Spend the night with **Whistler X-Country**

Ski and Hike (✆ 888/771-2382, 604/932-7711, www.whistler hikingcentre.com). They take care of ground and air transportation, food, camping supplies, backpacks, and overnights in a cabin. You get to experience a 1- to 3-day adventure, flying by floatplane to a high-altitude lake at 1,584m (5,200 ft.) in the Southern Chilcotin, 100km (62 miles) inland. An overnight trip is C$595 (US$371.85). **EcoMountain Tours** (✆ 800/925-4453, 604/913-2324, www. ecomountaintours.com) offers a full-day Whistler Nature Walk for C$99 (US$61.85) to Cheakamus Lake in Garibaldi Park. Led by naturalist Geza Vamos, this easy walk features a turquoise alpine lake, waterfalls, rainforest, and alpine flower meadows. **Whistler Outdoor Experience** (✆ 877/386-1888, 604/932-3389, www. whistleroutdoor.com) also offers easy nature walks to the 45m (150 ft.) Nairn Falls north of Whistler, as well as to Cheakamus Lake.

About an hour north of Whistler, you'll find Joffre Lakes, a wilderness area at the northern extremity of the Cascade Mountains. **Whistler Eco-Tours** (✆ 877-998-4900, 604/935-4900, www. whistlerecotours.com) is run by two brothers, Keenan and Elliot Moses, who now have a permit to take day hikes to the three turquoise subalpine lakes. Which one you choose to hike depends on your fitness level. You'll leave Whistler at 9am and return at 6pm for C$100 (US$62.50), children half-price. Ask for the Alpine Addiction tour.

 Bear Viewing with a Difference

Some 50 black bears make their home in the deep, old growth, coastal hemlock-cedar forests of Whistler Black-comb mountains. From May to July, bears wander along the open ski trails, grazing on clover, grass, and horsetail. From August to October, they fuel up for hibernation in the high-elevation timber-shrub forests, feeding on sugary huckle-berries. Researcher Michael Allen guides you along mountain access roads in a comfortable 4x4 to visit active bear dens, daybeds, and feeding sites. Viewer safety and avoiding disturbance to the bears always come first. Group size is limited to six. C$169 (US$105.60) for adults 17 to 59 years; C$159 (US$99.35) for youth aged 7 to 16 and seniors (60-plus). Bear viewing and mountain ecology tours are offered by Whistler Blackcomb (✆ 800-766-0449, 604/ 932-3434, www.whistlerblackcomb.com).

MOTORIZED TOURS Check out **Whistler Valley Trolley Tours** (© **604/932-7565,** www.glaciercoachlines.com) if you're tired of walking or simply want to know more about the history of Whistler and the out-of-the-way places it has to offer. Two-hour fun and informative trolley tours are ideal for the curious traveler, from May through October, at C$25 (US$15.60) for adults, C$21 (US$14.35) for youth/seniors. Courtesy pickup at Chateau Whistler 10 minutes prior to each tour. For something a little less sedate, even hair-raising, **Hummer Tours from Cougar Mountain at Whistler** (© **888/932-9998,** 604/932-4086, www.cougarmountain.ca) are new to Whistler. If you're not familiar with these rough, tough back-country vehicles, think Desert Storm, but replace the desert with granite outcroppings. Tours are C$109 (US$68).

LOCAL LAKES AND TRAILS Whistler's five lakes are within easy distance of the Village. Just north of the Village is **Lost Lake,** a great place for barbecues and swimming. Explore the **Lost Lake Trail,** starting from the north end of the Day Skier Parking Lot. Stick with the main trail to the lake, or explore some of its byways. Try an easy stroll for a relaxing picnic; hike or bike for more exercise. A five-minute drive north of the Village, you'll find glacier-fed (read: cold year-round) **Green Lake,** the only lake in the Valley that allows motorboats. South of the Village are **Alta, Nita** (pronounced *nee-ta*) and **Alpha** lakes with popular beaches, picnic sites, and beach volleyball courts. The **Valley Trail System** is a well-marked, paved trail that makes its way around much of Whistler. The trail starts on the west side of Highway 99 adjacent to the Whistler Golf Course and winds past quiet residential areas as well as golf courses, parks, and lakes.

HORSEBACK RIDING

Whistler River Adventures (© **888/932-3532,** 604/932-3532, www.whistlerriver.com) offers 2-hour trail rides along the Green River, through the forest, and across the Pemberton Valley from the 10-acre riverside **Adventure Ranch.** Drive yourself to the ranch in 35 minutes, or ask the company to arrange transportation for you (cost is extra). The 2-hour ride costs C$55 (US$34.35), with longer rides available on request. At its Green Lake site, **Whistler Outdoor Experience** (© **877/386-1888,** 604/932-3389, www.whistlerout door.com) lets you ride Thunder or Lightning, and other nice, friendly horses, through 4km (2.4 miles) of trails on their property. A 1-hour ride is C$40 (US$25), children 12 and under half-price. Pony rides for kids are C$20 (US$12.50).

TENNIS

Located in Village North with a perfect view of both mountains from the lounge, the **Whistler Racquet & Golf Resort** is open year-round at 4500 Northland Blvd. (© **604/932-1991,** www.whistler tennis.com). Public facilities include three indoor courts, seven outdoor courts, and a practice cage. Indoor courts are C$32 (US$20) per hour (rental rackets C$5) and outdoor courts are C$16 (US$10) per hour. Adult lessons vary depending on the caliber of the instructor, starting at C$50 (US$31.25) for an hour-long private lesson. Junior Tennis Sport camps (age 6 to 15 years) range from C$166 (US$103.75) for 5 days, 3 hours a day. If the courts aren't full, juniors can drop in to the camps for C$45 (US$28) a session. For all club usage, it's best to book 24 hours in advance (longer for the 5-day junior camps). Cool off after your game in the pool for C$12 (US$7.50). The tennis club at the luxurious **Fairmont Chateau Whistler Resort** (© **604/938-8000**) offers lessons to the public from June to September, for adults 18 and up. Director of tennis Gary Winter gives private lessons for C$60 (US$37.50) an hour. Two- to 3-day tennis camps start at C$225 (US$140.60). If you're a guest at the Chateau, you can play in its three outdoor courts for free. The hotel also offers tennis packages.

Whistler Parks and Recreation (© **604/935-7529**) offers four free public courts at the Myrtle Philip Community School, Meadow Park Sports Centre, in White Gold subdivision, and behind the Fairmont Chateau Whistler parking lot.

Moments Studio Visits

Visit an artist's home studio to get an insider's view of how year-round residents live and to buy local art. Prices are affordable, ranging from a few dollars for cards to several hundred dollars for a unique work of art. Commissions are invited.

Potter Vincent Massey and his wife Cheryl, a basket-maker (© **604/932-6455**), painter/printmaker Cori Ross (© **604/932-3473**), and painter Isobel MacLaurin (© **604/ 932-5324**) are happy to show you around their studio galleries. **The Masseys** have lived on the slopes of Rainbow Mountain since 1965, when Vincent established a large pottery studio. His works express traditional English and

Japanese methods of stoneware, including firing techniques of wood, salt, and raku. You'll find high-fired decorative stoneware art pieces, as well as functional ware such as bowls, casseroles, and teapots. Cheryl was inspired to weave after taking a weekend course, and now harvests rushes from the local lakes. Her basketry is also woven from Pacific kelp and western red cedar bark.

Cori Ross expresses Whistler's sensibility in flowery summer images and light-hearted winter ones, in smallish paintings and prints that make perfect mementos. To get to her studio, you pass by some older Whistler residences, including rustic chalets that harken back to the early days of this now "urban alpine" resort.

The exuberant **Isobel MacLaurin,** a longtime Whistler resident, lives in an A-frame cabin with an enviable view of Alpha Lake. The big surprise is her 65 sq. m (700 sq. ft.) studio gallery filled with bright paintings of flora, fauna, and people. Isobel also gives individual art lessons. Enjoy her colorful signage around the Valley Trail on Alta Road, at the Whistler Interpretive Forest, and at Green Lake.

7

Shopping from A to Z

Shopping in Whistler takes all sizes and forms. In fact, you could go to Whistler simply to shop, for anything from sportswear, fine clothing, and jewelry to quality First Nations art and the best chocolate in British Columbia.

There are six shopping areas: Whistler Village, Upper Village, Village North, Whistler Creekside, Function Junction, and Nesters. Quality is high, with few run-of-the-mill souvenir shops. Browsing is definitely encouraged and, by and large, the price range is appropriate for what you buy. Some boutiques cater to the higher end, while others offer more reasonably priced clothing, including souvenir sweatshirts, T-shirts, and fleece vests. You'll also find a selection of popular retail chain stores.

Tips Money Matters

Whistler does have end-of-the-season sales, which can shave as much as 40% off a product. All goods and services are subject to a 14% tax, some of which may be refundable. Look for the brochure "Tax Refund Centre for Non-Resident Tourists (Hotels and Goods)," available at accommodation reception desks, for the ins and outs of getting a tax rebate.

Free parking is available in the day lot at Blackcomb Way and Lorimer Road, a 5-minute walk to Whistler Village, Village North, and Upper Village. Stores are generally open daily from 10am to 9pm, but some open earlier and some close at 11pm. Since Whistler is not known for having street numbers, call ahead for hours and directions to get to a desired shop.

1 Shopping by Areas

Most people start their shopping explorations in **Whistler Village.** With its European panache, the Village is a car-free place to stroll and shop. You'll find a host of restaurants, cafes, and coffee shops so that you can easily stop for the pause that refreshes. Shop for souvenirs and gifts, contemporary art and First Nations carving and jewelry (see "Whistler's Art Galleries" below), upscale clothing for both sexes, sports equipment and accessories, apparel, bath and body products, and spa services (see "Incomparable Spas" below). Some hotels, such as the Westin Resort Hotel & Spa, Delta Whistler Resort, Pan Pacific Lodge, and Timberline Lodge, have indoor shopping malls. Stores are closely connected and easy to find within their area (see the "Where to Shop" map).

Construction of **Village North** began in the mid-1990s to complement Whistler Village. It's located on the left after you turn off Highway 99 onto Village Gate Boulevard. Conveniently located close to hotels, lodges, and condominium-style rentals, you'll find several shopping areas, including Whistler Marketplace, a mall with 2-hour free parking, a pharmacy, IGA grocery store, liquor store, post office, coffee shops and restaurants, and plenty of interesting shops. Market Pavilion/Tyndall Stone Lodge and Town Plaza also have a variety of stores. Throughout Village North, look for one-of-a-kind and artisan-made gifts, reputable art galleries representing Canadian and international artists, children's toys and candies, and sport accessories.

In the **Upper Village,** also called Blackcomb Base, you'll find clothing stores, art galleries, souvenir stores, and more. This area offers quality clothing, jewelry, crafts, gifts, and sports equipment. A visit to the Fairmont Chateau Whistler's row of specialty shops on the mezzanine level will give you an excuse to view the splendid touches of this fine hotel, including a dome ceiling painted with real gold.

You won't feel intimidated by **Whistler Creekside** services, which include two gas stations, grocery stores, pubs, and restaurants. The area is expanding and within a year or 2 will include two mega condo-hotels and way more restaurants, pubs, and retail shops. The Husky Gas Station, a Whistler landmark at the corner of Highway 99 and Lake Placid Road, will also be completely renovated by 2004.

Nesters is a small strip mall, 2km (1.24 miles) north of Whistler Village. It's an easy stop for a florist, laundromat, video rentals, and sports retail shop. **Nesters Market & Pharmacy** (7019 Nesters Rd., ⓒ 604/932-3545) is a handy grocery store with free parking. Place your grocery order before 2pm and it will be delivered to you that day. Open 8am to 9pm.

2 Shopping A to Z

BOOKS & MAGAZINES

Armchair Books. 4205 Village Square. ✆ **604/932-5557.** An accessible bookstore, this is the place to find guides, maps, and nature books to plan your Whistler adventure. For those quieter evenings, look here for plenty of fiction, non-fiction, and British Columbia and First Nations books. Also carries CDs, videos, and newspapers.

Bestsellers. 110-4295 Blackcomb Way ✆ **604/938-1235.** Sells only best-selling books as well as CDs, cassettes, videos, and audio equipment.

CHILDREN'S CLOTHES, TOYS & CANDIES

Bear Pause. 19-4314 Main St. ✆ **604/905-0121.** All bears meet here in the Town Plaza. Look for Winnie the Pooh, Steiff, Gund, Ty, Merrythought and their kin, as well as a variety of bear-related collectibles.

Fun for Kids Clothing. 48-4297 Mountain Square. ✆ **604/ 932-2115.** Clothing, swimwear, and shoes for tots through teens.

Going Nuts. 4250 Village Stroll. ✆ **604/932-4676.** Nuts and Belgian chocolate dominate.

Great Games & Toys. 112-4350 Lorimer. ✆ **604/932-2043.** Toys, puzzles, lava lamps, novelties, and hands-on fun.

The Great Glass Elevator Candy Shop. 115-4350 Lorimer. ✆ **604/935-1076.** In the Whistler Marketplace, this is childhood incarnate, with a thousand kinds of candy clamoring for attention. Also sells helium balloons and party favors.

Rocky Mountain Chocolate Factory. 4190 Springs Lane. ✆ **604/932-4100.** Chocolate, coffee, cocoa. Yummy, made fresh.

Rogers' Chocolates. 17-4304 Main St. ✆ **604/905-2462.** At the Town Plaza, this classic British Columbian candy shop stocks a mouth-watering selection of old-fashioned favorites, gift selections in tins and boxes, and chocolates the size of hockey pucks.

FASHIONS FOR MEN & WOMEN

Amos & Andes The Sweater & Dress Shop. 102-4321 Village Gate Blvd. ✆ **604/932-7202.** Located in the Credit Union Building across from Cow's, this shop stocks unique unisex hand-knit sweaters of cozy wool and dresses for any occasion. Look for Fresh Produce, Cornell Trading, and more.

C Whistler's Art Galleries

Perhaps the biggest surprise is the number of Whistler's art galleries: more than a dozen in all, plus local artists like potter Vincent Massey (© 604/932-6455) and painter/print-maker Cori Ross (© 604/932-3473), who will invite you to visit their home studios.

A gallery stroll shows up the variety of artists and styles. At the **adele-campbell Fine Art Gallery** (4050 Whistler Way in the lobby level of the Delta Whistler Resort, © 604/938-0887) many top BC artists are featured, with a wide collection of Whistler landscapes and soapstone sculpture. **The Whistler Art Gallery,** also at 4050 Whistler Way (© 604/938-3001), features Canadian and international paintings as well as sculpture in jade, marble, and bronze. **The Whistler Inuit Gallery,** at nearby 4090 Whistler Way (© 604/935-3999), showcases traditional and contemporary Inuit sculpture and Canadian art.

At least three galleries offer quality West Coast and Northwest First Nations art. If you're not familiar with this genre, it is well worth a visit. You'll instantly see why powerful First Nations works are so popular on the West Coast, with many homes displaying at least one piece, be it a print, carving, or jewelry. Visit **Black Tusk Gallery** at 101-4359 Main St. (© 604/905-5540). **Northwest Connection Native Art Gallery** at 2-4232 Sunrise Alley (© 604/932-4646), and **Freestyle Framing & Art Gallery** at 122B-4338 Main St. (© 604/932-4077) to learn more.

The Plaza Galleries in Village North at 22-4314 Main St. (© 604/938-6233) is noted for its vibrant works by the late actor Anthony Quinn, comic Red Skelton, and the child prodigy Jasmin, among many others. **The West Coast Gallery,** 123-4320 Sundial Crescent (© 604/935-0087), is a relative newcomer, with vibrant and eclectic works as well as handcrafted local and native jewelry, silverware, and jade. **Mountain Craft Gallery** at 101-4295 Blackcomb Way (© 604/932-5001) highlights Canadian artists, including oil paintings and glass beadwork. **Art Junction@Function** at 1050 Millar Creek Rd. (© 604/938-9000) showcases contemporary British Columbia artists.

Biggest Little Shirt House in Whistler. 4182 Springs Lane. ℂ **604/938-9740.** Unisex and children's T-shirts, jackets, sweatshirts, neck warmers, gloves, and hats.

Driscoll's Sweaters. 4050 Whistler Way. ℂ **604/938-6687.** Sweaters, jackets, sweatshirts, and gift items.

Eddie Bauer. 116-4295 Blackcomb Way. ℂ **604/938-3268.** Casual sporty clothes and accessories for men and women.

Edin Boutique. 103A-4295 Blackcomb Way. ℂ **604/938-9990.** Elegant clothing for women that's chic, casual, and unexpected.

The Escape Route North. 113-4350 Lorimer. ℂ **604/938-3228.** A great line of outdoor clothing and equipment.

The Gap. 5-4308 Main St. ℂ **604/938-6364.** US chain of youthful, sporty, casual clothes.

The Gift of Golf Shop. 4599 Chateau Blvd. ℂ **604/938-2206.** Men's and ladies' golf wear, equipment, accessories, and casual wear.

The Hat Gallery. 103B-4295 Blackcomb Way. ℂ **604/938-6695.** Located in Whistler Village Centre next to the pedestrian bridge, this is the headquarters for headgear. Hat Lady Annie Erwin displays an array of hats that include Stetsons, berets, driving caps, Australian outback hats, animal novelty numbers, snoods, and the ultimate accessory, handmade hatpins.

Horstman Trading Company. 4555 Blackcomb Way. ℂ **604/938-7725.** Beside the Chateau Whistler at the base of Blackcomb, the shop carries men's and women's casual wear, from swimwear and footwear to polar-fleece vests and nylon jacket shells.

Inside Out Boutique. 30-4314 Main St. ℂ **604/932-2145.** In Whistler Town Plaza. If your unders couldn't hack it on the slopes, this super little boutique will come to your rescue. It carries a full range of bra sizes in Lejaby, Triumph, and Canadian-made Elita, among others, in big-city stylings. To cover your bottom half, there are thongs as well as more capacious granny panties, snugglies, and tights. Sells great pajamas and loungewear, perfect for lolling by the fireplace. The store squeezes a lot of great fashion into a very tiny space.

Le Chateau. 104-4338 Main St. ℂ **604/932-3702.** Canadian chain of trendy, fun, and affordable youth-oriented fashions.

Milania Leather. 118-4295 Blackcomb Way. ℂ **604/905-4911.** Leather jackets for men and women, Whistler souvenir T-shirts, and accessories.

Mount Cashmere. 125-4090 Whistler Way. ℂ **604/905-7729.** In the Westin Resort & Spa, this shop offers exquisitely soft cashmere in a tempting range of shapes and styles: choose from cardigans and turtlenecks, V-necks and round-necks, pashminas, capes, scarves, and gloves.

Open Country Whistler. 4599 Chateau Blvd. ℂ **604/938-9268.** Classic fashions by Liz Claiborne, Jones New York, and Calvin Klein.

Roots. 4229 Village Stroll. ℂ **604/938-0058.** Canadian-designed casual clothes, including leather, Whistler wear, accessories, and a children's line.

Rumpleshirtskins. E-4227 Village Stroll. ℂ **604/932-2040.** Whistler souvenir T-shirts, sweatshirts, jackets.

Seasons of Whistler. 4242A Village Stroll. ℂ **604-938-0092.** Great hats, in unique cloche and dressy styles. Creative sweaters, especially if you like cats, and smooth red furry hiking boots, a concept that somehow works.

Snowflake. 4599 Chateau Blvd. ℂ **604/938-2019.** Features exquisite knit fur garments and accessories for women.

Willy's Suave Threads. 125-4295 Blackcomb Way (ℂ **604/938-9900),** 4314 Main St. ℂ **604/938-9334.** Men's and women's street gear, accessories, and baseball caps.

GIFTS & SOUVENIRS

Carlbergs. 4325 Sunrise Alley. ℂ **604/932-3554.** Pottery, jewelry, pewter, stationery, and other giftware, plus home accessories and souvenirs.

Christmas at Whistler. 4293 Mountain Square. ℂ **604/932-3518.** Christmas ornaments, decorations, and gifts.

Cow's Whistler. 102-4295 Blackcomb Way. ℂ **604/938-9822.** Carries original-design T-shirts, seats, and souvenirs (cow-based, of course), and the ultimate cow product, ice cream.

For KeepSakes. 400-4241 Village Stroll. ℂ **604/932-3900.** Cards and giftware, jewelry, and bath products.

49th Parallel. 6-4314 Main St. ℂ **604/905-0997.** Custom printing, fleece, goggles, sweatshirts, and golf shirts.

Lotus Art Supplies. 121-4338 Main St. ℭ **604/938-0055.** A cute shop with tools of the trade for the artist and crafter, special paper, cards, plus exotic small gifts from faraway places.

Memories of Whistler. 4249 Village Stroll. ℭ **604/932-6439.** Canadiana: souvenirs, sweatshirts, and gift items.

Mountain Blooms Florist. 122-4340 Lorimer. ℭ **604/932-2599.** Fresh flowers, plants, giftware, and helium balloons.

Mountain Spirit Gift Gallery. 123-4090 Whistler Way (Westin Resort & Spa). ℭ **604/932-1878.** Soapstone, jade, and wood carvings, ammolite, ivory, plush toys, delicate Hummels, and wooden bowls and plates by master wood turner and carver George Berkenpas.

New Jersey's Clothing Co. 5-4122 Village Green. ℭ **604/938-0904.** Canadian T-shirts, sweatshirts, hats, fleece, and souvenirs.

Oh Yes Whistler! 28-4314 Main St. ℭ **604/905-4490.** Carries genuinely Canadian T-shirts and a selection of what the *L.A. Times* called the "classiest souvenirs in the world."

Snowberries of Whistler. 4241 Village Stroll. ℭ **604/932-3778.** Native art and British Columbia crafts, Canadian jade and soapstone carvings, pottery, and folk art.

Spirit of the North. 4299B Mountain Square. ℭ **604/932-5455.** Duty-free shopping, plus a large selection of Canadian souvenirs, food, and clothing.

Svepol Crystal. 112-4368 Main St. ℭ **604/938-1688.** An excellent collection of one-of-a-kind Bohemian crystal, crystal jewelry, and crystal animals.

Whacks of Whistler. 4222 Village Square. ℭ **604/905-0011.** Casual souvenir clothing and lots more.

Zaveri The Jewel of Whistler. 203 Mountain Square. ℭ **604/932-1100.** Jewelry and gift items.

HOUSEWARES, FURNISHINGS & ANTIQUES

The Daily Planet. 1-1030 Millar Creek. ℭ **604/938-6336.** Located in Function Junction, and packed with fun, functional items both new and used. Discover original art, antiques, retro pieces, and rare antiques from Persian carpets and antique sleighs to dinosaur bones. Quality used furniture, original art, cool stuff.

Loral Furniture. 4-1208 Alpha Lake Rd. ℭ **604/932-1211.** Located in the atypical industrial park Function Junction, Loral specializes in log, pine, and driftwood furniture. Order a piece of furniture from a sample and it will be made up for you in BC and shipped to your home. You'll also find accessories like Kootenay Forge River Rock Lamps, and ceramic bowls, platters, and other items by potter Penny E. Martyn.

Skitch. 4224 Village Square. ✆ **604/938-1781.** Great selection of gifts and accessories for the home.

Whistler Hardware & Gifts. 101-4305 Skiers Approach. ✆ **604/ 932-3863.** Hardware, housewares, toys, sleds, and key cutting.

Whistler Kitchen Works. 116-4350 Lorimer. ✆ **604/938-1110.** A favorite with the locals in Whistler Marketplace, this shop is loaded with an exhaustive supply of teapots, mugs, local pottery and Italian ceramics, aprons, table linens, knives, and other kitchenware. Great for gifts, too.

JEWELRY

Henry Birks and Sons. 114-4295 Blackcomb Way. ✆ **604/ 935-1818.** Found near Starbucks in Whistler Village Centre, Birks carries on a well-established Canadian tradition of fine jewelry and gifts.

Keir Fine Jewelry. 4321 Village Gate Blvd. ✆ **604/932-2944.** Located in the North Shore Credit Union Building, and featuring Canadian diamonds and unusual, handcrafted designs.

Van Raniga Jewellers & Designers. 203-4297 Mountain Square. ✆ **604/938-1100.** Worth a trip upstairs in the Delta Whistler Resort to see some of the world's finest skiing and snowflake jewelry. Jewelers, gemologists, designers, and goldsmiths team up to create award-winning masterpieces inspired by classic art and nature.

 Insight into Canadian Diamonds

If you're interested in buying Canadian diamonds, here are a few tips. Distinctive white color (H) diamonds are both rare and in great demand. The Maple Leaf™ beauties are 1/3 carat or larger and have a laser-inscribed Maple Leaf and identification number. Three certificates of authenticity must accompany this diamond, from mine to retail. The worldwide demand for Canadian diamonds is high because they're from conflict-free mines. The Ekati Diamond Mine T (www.ekati.ca) is by value the world's fourth largest mine. Opened in 1998, it's located 200km (124 miles) south of the Arctic Circle, in Canada's Northwest Territories. Forty percent of its skilled workforce is First Nations. Another Canadian brand is Sirius, or Polar Bear Diamonds (www.polarbeardiamonds.com). The genuine diamond laser-engraving has a polar bear facing left, with four legs visible. A numbered certificate of authenticity stating that it's a Canadian Ideal Cut will be included with your purchase. These are all stunningly beautiful stones, and the true-life story of the Canadian geologist Charles Fipke who discovered the Ekati property is a great adventure, well told in *Fire into Ice* by Vernon Keir Fine Jewelry, and Van Raniga Jewellers & Designers.

LIQUOR & CIGARS

Hoz's Cold Beer & Wine Store. 2129 Lake Placid Rd. ℂ **604/932-5926.** Located in Whistler Creekside.

Marketplace Liquor Store (BC Liquor Stores). 101-4360 Lorimer. ℂ **604/932-7251.** Like the Village Liquor Store below, this province-run outlet has a wide selection of local and international products.

Vancouver Cigar Company. 31-4314 Main St. ℂ **604/932-6099.** Selection of premium cigars (Cuban cigars a specialty), tobacco products, and accessories.

Village Liquor Store (BC Liquor Stores). 4211 Village Square. ℂ **604/932-5050.**

Whistler Cigar Company. 4557 Blackcomb Way (in Le Chamois). ℂ **604/905-2423.**

SKIN CARE

The Body Shop. 4222 Village Square. ℂ **604/932-2639.** Skin care, hair care, and cosmetics inspired by nature.

Escents Aromatherapy. 20-4314 Main St. ℂ **604/905-2955.** A BC-based company producing quality essential oils, diffusers, incense, candles, and aromatherapy-related gifts.

Fiber Options. 1-4118 Village Green. ℭ **604/905-3181.** Earth-friendly cosmetics, wood products, and clothing.

Lush Handmade Cosmetics. 10-4308 Main St. ℭ **604/932-5445.** Fresh, handmade cosmetics and soaps, including bath bombs, vegetable soap, and flying saucers.

 Incomparable Spas

Therapeutic or indulgent? Spas abound in Whistler and they are deliciously sybaritic. Start with a basic massage from a Registered Massage Therapist. The province's training standards are the highest in North America, consisting of 3,000 hours of rigorous instruction for the RMT who will treat you.

Spas compete for clients with exotic, luxurious treatments, some of which are highly unusual. At the **Fairmont Chateau Whistler Spa and Health Club** (ℭ 604/938-8000) in the Upper Village, nothing can compare to the Ayurvedic Bhindi Shirodana, a 90-minute renewal by a highly trained practitioner, pampering the weary with custom blends of oils based on a 5,000-year-old tradition. Ayurvedic is based on the three elements of air, fire, and water. The warmed oil flows onto your body, followed by warmed towels, and then all your cares are massaged away. Arrive a bit early to fill out a helpful questionnaire for Eileen Flett, Ayurvedic therapist and part-owner of the spa. This treatment is popular, so book early. The cost is C$190 (US$119). Sports enthusiasts and sybarites alike will also welcome a deep-tissue massage in the Chateau's elegant slate and limestone surroundings.

An equally sumptuous spa, **Avello Spa & Health Club** (ℭ 604/935-3444), can be found in the Westin Resort & Spa. Signature treatments include the Vichy Shower Treatment, for C$95 (US$60), similar to having buckets of warm rain cascading over your body, and the Hot Rock Massage, for C$220 (US$137.50), poetically described as having trails of heated stones flowing on the body until you sink into the table grounded in mother earth.

Whistler Body Wrap (ℭ 604/932-4710), Suite 210 St. Andrews House, Whistler Village next to the Keg, offers a full range of beauty and body care, including sports massage, deep tissue, shiatsu, reflexology, relaxation, and aromatherapy. C$60 to C$160 (US$37.50 to US$100). **Whistler Therapeutic Centre** (✆ 604/938-4943), located in Whistler Village Square, has a full-body clay mask for C$90 (US$56.25), among other treatments. If you're on Whistler Mountain, you may also find therapists from **Blue Highways Shiatsu & Massage** (✆ 604/938-0777). Sample massages on the mountain go for C$1 (US$.60) a minute, up to 10 minutes, by way of introduction to the company. Permanent clinics are in Market Pavilion above the 7-Eleven, and in the Coast Whistler Hotel. Treatments at **Esperanza Day Spa** (✆ 604/905-4855, 208-4368 Main St. in the 7-Eleven building) range from C$85 (US$53.10) for a 1-hour massage to C$180 (US$112.50) for the self-renewal face and body treatment including a body scrub, massage, scalp and hair treatment, and mini-facial.

SPORTS CLOTHES, ACCESSORIES & EQUIPMENT

Affinity Sports. 114-4557 Blackcomb Way (in Le Chamois). ✆ 604/938-1743. Local wear, T-shirts, and ski and snowboard outfits.

Beach or Bust. 123-4340 Lorimer. ✆ 604/932-7505. Bathing suits and beachwear.

Blackcomb Ski & Sport. 4553 Blackcomb Way. ✆ 604/938-7788. Equipment rentals plus logo wear, sunglasses, and accessories.

Can-Ski. Four locations: Can-Ski Sportshop at 100-4253 Village Stroll (✆ 604/938-7755), Can-Ski Glacier Lodge at 4573 Chateau Blvd. (✆ 604/938-7744), Can-Ski Creekside at 2051 Lake Placid Rd. (✆ 604/905-2160), and Can-Ski North in Deer Lodge at 32-4314 Main St. (✆ 604/938-7432). Full-service ski stops feature The North Face Summit Shop, plus a selection of summer gear and equipment.

Cougar Mountain at Whistler. 36-4316 Main St. ✆ 604/932-4086. Winter clothing accessories, backcountry wear, fly and tackle equipment, and snowshoes.

Escape Route North. 113-4350 Lorimer. ℂ **604/938-3228.** Mountaineering, alpine touring, ice and rock climbing equipment, and outerwear.

Evolution. 8-4122 Village Green. ℂ **604/932-2967.** Accessories, clothing, and service for snowboarders.

Eyes on Whistler. 11-4599 Chateau Blvd. ℂ **604/938-2831.** Sunglasses, prescription glasses, and contact lenses.

Helly Hansen Store. 4090 Whistler Way (Westin Resort & Spa), ℂ **604/932-0142,** and 108-4295 Blackcomb Way, ℂ **604/932-0143.** Outerwear, skiwear, Ray Bans, and other accessories.

Horstman Trading Co. 4555 Blackcomb Way. ℂ **604/938-7725.** Logo wear, casual clothes, swimwear, and footwear. Exclusive Bogner skiwear collection.

McCoo's Excessive Accessories. 4198 Springs Lane. ℂ **604/932-2842.** Ski and snowboard equipment and accessories. Also **McCoo's Too.** 111-4295 Blackcomb Way. ℂ **604/938-9954.** Clothes for skiing and snowboarding.

Mountain Shop. 202-4283 Mountain Square. ℂ **604/932-2203.** Outer wear, ski clothing, casual wear, and accessories.

The Penalty Box/Whistler Blades. 118-4368 Main St. ℂ **604/938-9667.** Logo wear, hockey jerseys, pants, men's and women's casual clothes, and skater-punk–style shoes.

SMS Camps and Clothing. 201-1390 Alpha Lake Rd. ℂ **604/905-4421.** Small snowboard clothing outlet, featuring jackets and pants designed in Whistler, with last year's styles at a discount.

Snow Covers Sports. 126-4340 Lorimer. ℂ **604/905-4100.** Ski shop selling all top brands of jackets, pants, and other ski accessories.

Sportstop. 4112 Golfers Approach. ℂ **604/932-5495.** Ski clothing and apparel, after-ski boots, cross-country ski boots, binding and clothing, trail and light hiking shoes, ice hockey and ski equipment, and swimsuits.

Surefoot Sports. 126-4295 Blackcomb Way. ℂ **604/938-1663.** Ski boots, hiking boots, orthotics, as well as custom boot fitting and ski boot accessories.

Westbeach Snowboard Skateboard & Surf Shop. 119-4350 Lorimer. ℂ **604/932-2526.** Summer and snow sport accessories plus outerwear, street wear, and children's brand names.

Whistler Optik. 124-4295 Blackcomb Way. ✆ **604/938-0744.** Prescription eyewear and lab, sunglasses, binoculars, and swim goggles.

Wild Willies Ski Club. 101-2011 Innsbruck Dr. ✆ **604/938-8032.** 7011/7017 Nesters Rd. ✆ **604/938-8036.** 101-4321 Village Gate Blvd., ✆ **604/938-9836.** Yes, there really is a Willie. Owner William Lamond celebrated the opening of his third store in mid-December 2001 in the Village, in addition to his Creekside outlet on Innsbruck Drive and one in Nesters Square. Known for its fitting expertise and rental equipment for skiing and snowboarding, Wild Willies also has boutiques with a wide selection of casual wear, including ski suits, board wear, Gore-Tex, micro-fleece, gloves, long underwear, goggles, children's wear, helmets, and more.

8

Whistler After Dark

Whistler doesn't curl up in front of a fireplace after a hard day outdoors. Starting with après ski and continuing on to the club scene, there's a choice for anyone with an eye to staying up later than 9pm. Depending on your age and adaptability, enjoy everything from high-energy dance clubs to low-key lounges. Clubs promote variety with theme nights during the week, including house, hip-hop, techno, and trance. Check with **Pique newsmagazine,** a free local paper, and the **Whistler Question** bi-weekly tabloid for bands playing in town. Some name acts even make Whistler their Canadian debut.

1 A Touch of Class

Nightlife in Whistler isn't all sweaty dancers and beer by the bottle. Boosted by community support, you can now see a play, attend a concert or lecture, watch folk dancing or ballet, or attend a First Nations ceremonial presentation. The June 2001 completion of the multi-faceted 6,858 sq. m (22,500 sq. ft.) **Maurice Young Millennium Place (© 604/935-8410,** Box Office © 604/935-8418) at 4335 Blackcomb Way is the culmination of the community's 35-year dream. With a 250-tiered seat concert hall, MY Place (as it's known locally) hosts theatrical and dance performances, concerts, children's performances, community events, and spiritual services. Samples of entertainment include a hot jazz series, with adult tickets for C$20 (US$12.50) and students for C$10 (US$6.25), or a chamber music orchestra playing intimate selections from Mozart, Tchaikovsky, and DeBussy's En Bateau Suite for piano with four hands. For children, there are such shows as a comic version of *Cinderella* performed by **The Whistler Players.** The theatre doubles as venue for Warren Miller's ski mania movies, such as *Cold Fusion, The Power of Snow,* with adult tickets for C$9 (US$5.50) and students for C$7 (US$4.35).

2 Après Ski

When every muscle in your body screams for mercy after hours on the slopes, an après-ski break is just what the doctor ordered before you hit the hot tub. Whether your choice is a cold beer or glass of wine, you won't be at a loss for an après venue. Whistler is well put together with dozens of after-hours spots just waiting for you to hobble in and flop down for the break that refreshes. Après bars and lounges are spread throughout Whistler. Some, like the **Crystal Lounge** (© **604-938-1081**), located in the Crystal Lodge, and **Brandy's Lounge** at the Keg at the Mountain at the Whistler Village Inn (© **604/932-5151**), are low-key spots in Whistler Village. You can't miss **Citta's** lively outdoor patio (© **604/932-4177**), set on a significant corner on the Village Square just a short walk from the gondolas. **Tapley's Neighbourhood Pub** (© **604/932-4011**), across from the Conference Centre in Whistler Village, is a full-kitchen sports bar catering mostly to locals. Whatever your mood, here are a few of the more than 30 après (and even après-après) ski spots, presented by location throughout the resort.

WHISTLER SIDE

Black's Pub & Original Ristorante   Both a pub and a restaurant, Black's offers family dining in its downstairs restaurant, as well as an upstairs pub. If you head upstairs for an après-ski beverage, you'll be welcomed by a choice of 99 international beers plus 40 brands of scotch. There's also a great mountain view from a window seat, and a good menu. A variety of pastas and pizza is offered nightly. Occasional live entertainment. Operates from 7am to 1am daily, with "Appy Hour" Sunday to Friday, 3pm to 7pm. Located in the Westbrook Hotel in Whistler Village at the base of the Village gondolas (© **604/932-6408,** www.goodtimes@whistler blackspub.com).

Cinnamon Bear Bar   Sink into the oversized comfy chairs and couches and it may be hours before you make it back to your hotel room. From the life-sized carved cinnamon-colored bear outside to the backgammon tables, pool table, and fireplace inside, the atmosphere here is very pleasant. On the menu is a heaping appetizer platter with hot wings, vegetable spring rolls, Jalapeno poppers, chicken fingers, tortilla chips, and two dips. Sandwiches include steak and chicken items as well as the Reuben, made with Montreal smoked meat, thinly sliced with sauerkraut and Swiss cheese on dark rye bread. Sports fan will enjoy the big-screen television. Live entertainment. Open 11am to 1am Monday to Saturday; 11am to midnight on Sunday. Located in the Delta Whistler Hotel (© **604/932-1982**).

The Dubh Linn Gate   The prestigious 2002 Zagat restaurant guide listed the Dubh Linn Gate as one of the best dining experiences in the world, based on customer satisfaction ratings of food, service, and value. This is a cozy Irish-style pub where people relax and linger over tasty Irish stew and the best halibut'n'chips. Add a choice of 20 beers on tap and 60 whiskies. The 20-ounce pints of beer are formidable. A pint of the legendary dark Guinness beer goes down well with live music offerings. It helps that the manager comes from an Irish family that counts seven generations in the pub business. You'll be talking with a hint of the Irish before the night's out in this lively Celtic ambiance, with the old ancestors looking down from oil portraits. You may have to wait for a seat, as the place is popular with visitors and resort workers alike. Open 7am for breakfast until 1am (Sunday at midnight). Located in the Pan Pacific Lodge at the base of Whistler and Blackcomb Village gondolas (© **604/905-4047,** www.dubhlinngate.com).

Garibaldi Lift Company   Referred to simply as GLC, this is a convenient favorite for skiers off Whistler and Blackcomb mountain runs. Weekend visitors from Vancouver crowd the place en route to their ski cabins. Find a seat at the windows for a floor-to-ceiling view of Whistler Mountain's Olympic ski run on one side and Whistler Village on the other. Not to be missed is the sultry "Sex Cheese," a concoction of four cheeses served with Armenian flat bread, or any GLC burger. The atmosphere is fun and friendly all around. Open at 11:30am until midnight. Located above the Whistler Gondola building (© **604/905-2220,** www.whistlerblackcomb.com). Some cover charges for live music events.

Longhorn Saloon   Ski right into the bar and patio when the lifts shut down at 3:30pm. The Longhorn is a wild, noisy, crowded traditional Canadian pub where it's said to be impossible to fall down drunk, because there's no room to fall. With a powerful sound system, a small dance floor, good-looking revelers, and friendly service, as well as live bands on occasion, the Longhorn quenches everyone's thirst with lots of cold beer (and some of it ends up on the floor). Word is that Longhorn serves more beer per square foot in winter than any other bar in Canada. Waitresses finesse their way through the crowds with trays of beer, or Longhorn coffees, a mystical mix of butter-ripple cream schnapps, Kahlua, and coffee. Open from 11am to 1am. Located less than 50m (165 ft.) from the Whistler and Blackcomb Gondolas (© **604/932-5999,** www.longhorn.net).

UPPER VILLAGE

Mallard Bar   With a fabulous view of the mountains, and located inside one of Whistler's eminently classy hotels, the Mallard Bar is one of the most civilized après-ski bars on earth. Featuring two firepits on the patio for après-ski and nightly dining. Live entertainment daily. An "Alpine Tea" is served between 2pm and 4pm (like an English high tea, alpine style), with everything from steak sandwiches to beluga caviar. You can even smoke in an enclosed indoor cigar room. Open 11am to 1am (except for Sunday, when it closes at 12 midnight). Located in the Fairmont Chateau Whistler (© **604/938-8000,** wwwfairmont.com).

Merlin's Bar & Grill   Part of the fun at Merlin's is its popular theme parties. If you're into costumes and likeable entertainment, ask when the next event happens. Any day, Merlin's is the quintessential après-ski bar. You'll be part of a younger crowd, likely to rub shoulders with athletic types like visiting sport stars or ski and snowboard instructors. Accent notes are live music, stage acts, and film premieres. The patio, come spring, is crowded and deservedly so. The nachos are out of this world. Open 11am to 1am. Located at the base of Blackcomb Mountain (© **604/938-7735,** www.beer.com).

Monk's Grill   A great place to people watch, appealing to the 30-something crowd. Order snacks or a light dinner in the bar, or visit the upscale dining room (but leave your ski boots behind). The music is lively but not overpowering and the mountain view of Blackcomb is sublime. Monk's may be the only the place in Whistler that doesn't scream mountain chalet with its decor. Opens weekdays 11:30am to 10pm; weekends 11am to 10pm. Located at the base of Blackcomb Mountain (© **604/932-9677,** www.monksgrill@whistlerweb.com).

WHISTLER CREEKSIDE

Dusty's Bar & BBQ   The old Dusty's was built in 1965 with a couple of double-wide trailers at the base of the original Whistler gondola at Creekside. The mascot was a ride-'em-cowboy bucking bronco named Dusty, and for the locals it was a second home. The bull is gone, as are the trailers. The new Dusty's is a two-storey lodge-style stone-and-timber bar with a well-worn, casual look, thanks to savvy designers who brought in distressed wood and mismatched chairs to ease the shock to the old-time skiers who frequent the bar. Dusty's barbecued ribs alone are worth the trek to Creekside. Staff is friendly and helpful, the atmosphere isn't hurried, and stellar live music hits the spot. For takeout and quick noshes, there's Dusty's Backside under the Gondola. Open 11am to midnight Sunday through Thursday; and to 1am Friday and Saturday. Located at Whistler Creekside at the base of the Creekside Gondola (© **604/905-2171**).

Hoz's Pub   Where the locals go. Hoz's is a casual hangout near the base of Whistler Mountain in Creekside. Food is what you'd expect and what you'd like if you're young and living on one main meal a day. Pizza with an international touch comes with chorizo, bacon, mushrooms, red onion, sundried tomatoes, and basil pesto. Chicken and ribs, and the traditional killer of a Quebec dish known as poutine (fries topped with cheddar, Monterey Jack, Edam cheese, and old-style gravy), are also on the menu. Open 11am to midnight. Located at 2129 Lake Placid Rd., Whistler Creekside (© **604/932-5940,** www.hozspub.com).

3 Nightclubs

The Boot Pub   A raucous, youthful place where beer reigns supreme after an intense day on the slopes. The place to meet visitors and foreign workers living on a shoestring while having the time of their unfettered lives. The decor is living-room trash, the atmosphere maxed-out casual. Check out the theme nights, such as Sunday punk music night, and DJ Hoffa with Das Boot Ballet exotic dancing until 1am on Tuesday, Wednesday, and Friday nights. Thursday is local jam night and Saturday's live bands attract the hordes. Opens at 3pm andcloses at 1pm on Sunday; 2pm to midnight on Mondays and Tuesdays; 3pm to midnight on Wednesdays; 3pm to 2am on Thursdays; 3 pm to 1am on Fridays; and 3pm to 2am on Saturdays. Cover charge C$1 to C$5 or more (US$.60 to US$3.10). Located 1km (.62 mile) north of the Village, just off Highway 99. Make a left on Nancy Greene Drive (© **604/932-3338,** www.thebootpub.com). Free parking.

Buffalo Bill's Bar and Grill   Here's one that's ever popular with the 30-something crowd. Bill's has pool tables, a big-screen TV, ski simulators, and dancing nightly on a full dance floor. The music is retro Top 40, with occasional live bands. Watch your favorite sports on 13 video screens. Bill's also features infamous stagette parties with women outnumbering men two to one. The menu features

Montreal-style smoked meat sandwiches and burgers. Open 2pm until 2am, except on Sundays until 1pm. Cover charge from Thursday to Sunday ranges from C$3 to C$12 (US$1.85 to US$7.50). Located across from the Conference Centre in Whistler Village (© **604/932-6613,** www.buffalobills.whistler.net).

Garfinkel's Nightclub   The cut-off age for the hip crowd at Garfinkel's can reach as high as 30, but if you're older and you can fake it, more power to you. Recent renovations have spruced up the place, including the addition of the biggest stage in town. You'll recognize the big names on the touring circuit playing here. Theme nights include Thursday Local's Night, voted the best Locals Night 10 years running, with resident DJs Stoli and Erin, and Fresh Fridays with DJ R3. Open from 8:30pm to 2am. The cover charge on Thursdays is C$2 (US$1.25), and goes to local charities. Weekends it's C$5 (US$3.10). Located on the north side of the bridge that separates Whistler Village and Village North (© **604/932-2323,** www.garfswhistler.com).

Maxx Fish   Dark. Huge. Crowded. Booted into life by some of the hottest DJs around, Maxx Fish caters to the 18- to 22-year-old crowd 7 nights a week. You might end up sitting next to a famous local athlete at the bar. Party night is every night, with hot DJs including DJ Keph's "mixed bag of traxx" on Saturday night, DJ Spin Cat with sexy funk music on Mondays, and Matt the Alien + Kilo Cee with hip-hop on Wednesdays. Open Monday through Saturday 9pm to 2am; Sunday 9pm to 1am. Located in the Village Square below the Amsterdam Cafe (© **604/932-1904,** www.maxxfish.com).

Moe Joe's   A newcomer to the club scene, casual and relaxed Moe Joe's quickly became a locals' hangout. It's noted for its funky mix of hip-hop and house music. On Tuesday's disco night, you can win a prize as best disco dancer, incentive enough if you're in the 28-year-old range. Weekends feature live bands. Open 9pm to 2am. Cover charge C$3 to C$5 weekends (US$1.85 to US$3.10). Located off the main Village Square, across from Buffalo Bill's (© **604/935-1152,** www.moejoes.com).

Savage Beagle   Caters to the 30-something crowd with two floors of goodies, including a pleasantly laidback lounge upstairs (ask for one of their smooth martinis or fresh-squeezed juices) and dance floor below. Part of the enduring attraction is its outstanding selection of beer and bar drinks (it has the most extensive back bar in town). The crowded dance floor and 120-decibel sound system account for the other part of the attraction. Special dance nights like Tuesday's hip-hop with DJ Seanski spin the best. Opens at 8pm, closes at 2am. Cover charge is C$5 to C$10 (US$3.10 to US$6.25). No cover if you come early. Located in the heart of Whistler Village (© **604/938-3337,** www.savagebeagle.com).

Tommy Africa's   Another satisfyingly dark and loud club, with crowds of 18- to 22-year-olds. With some 15 years under its belt, Tommy's has seen its share of wild and crazy nights. Go-go girls still grace the stage, hip-hugger shorts and boots intact. International DJs ensure that the club stays fresh. Theme nights include Monday's 1980s retro boogie offerings in a setting that has been described as equal parts bomb shelter and Hawaiian luau. *Skiing* magazine called this the best place to shake your booty in Whistler. Opens at 9pm. Located beneath the Pharmasave at the entrance to the Main Village (© **604/932-6090,** www.tommyafricas.com).

9

Whistler for Kids

Kid friendly is what Whistler is all about. You may even see a **Kid Friendly** sticker in a restaurant or business window, proof that the place has officially passed inspection by the best experts possible—kids themselves. Sticker or not, local businesses, including Blackcomb and Whistler mountains, have families in mind, some with discounts and freebies to keep costs down.

A decade ago, the resort realized it would need to attract families to ensure year-round success. It has pumped up the volume (figuratively speaking) to entice and entertain children and youth. Just about any attraction, tour, package, or program can accommodate children. Others have been designed with children in mind, including old-fashioned sleigh rides and special "kids only" ski lessons.

Summer and winter are naturally the busiest seasons in the resort. But spring and fall are not entirely neglected. Whistler and Blackcomb mountains offer off-season programs for those 18 months to 12 years, run by trained counselors and instructors. Activities for children 4 and under include nature walks, visits to the puppy daycare and firehall, and arts and crafts. For the 5 to 12 set, nature hikes, treks to Lost Lake, gondola sightseeing, swimming, outdoor group games, and arts and crafts are offered. Full-day fare is C$68 (US$42.50), half-day is C$40 (US$25). While some programs and packages may not be available in the off-seasons, don't forget that Whistler is all about nature, and nature is there 365 days a year. Call the **Whistler Activity and Information Centre** (© 604/932-2394) year-round for more information and to book children's activities in the resort. For overall information, check with **Tourism Whistler** at www.tourismwhistler.com.

To feel more at home in Whistler, visiting children can swim or ice skate with the locals at the **Meadow Park Sports Centre** © 604/935-7529 (see more information in this chapter). The **Myrtle Philip Community School,** at 6195 Lorimer Road in Whistler Cay subdivision © **604/935-8371,** is another family-oriented multi-purpose facility with a variety of year-round programs. Try **Kids on the Go,** a drop-in where local and visiting children between 6 and 12 years get to meet each other on weekdays from 2:30pm to 6pm during the school year, for C$7 per day, C$9 on Thursdays (US$ 4.35, US$5.60). Games, crafts, cooking, out-trips, and more keep kids interested. Weekend courses such as Recyclable Art are fun and educational for 6- to 12-year-olds. Or visit with the big man himself on Super Santa Days for 3- to 5-year-olds just before Christmas.

For independent travel with children, swimming, walking, biking, and picnicking are just some of the things your family will enjoy without breaking the bank. Get to know the five Whistler Valley lakes and the Valley Trail. You can even take in a first-run family matinee for C$6.50 (US$4.05) to catch movies such as *Harry Potter* or *Lord of the Rings* at the 300-seat Dolby surround Rainbow Theatre ℂ **604/932-2422.** Then there is the highly recommended **Whistler WinterStart Festival,** held early in December to kick off the winter season (see below for more information). Because WinterStart is held just before the very busiest weeks of Christmas and New Year's, prices are significantly lower.

Many families choose to rent condos, townhouses, or homes to save time and money and to make it easier on their children by cooking at home. Others enjoy **Whistler's many hotels** with surprises in store for visiting families. Legends (ℂ **800/799-3258,** 604/938-9999), a new lodge in Whistler Creekside, offers a families-only hot tub, as well as heated outdoor swimming pool, media room with daily showings of child-oriented videos, and a playroom full of toys. The Westin Resort & Spa Whistler (ℂ **800/WESTIN-1**) offers special services, activities, and amenities for children 4 to 12 with Whistler Kid's Club. Hotels may have babysitting services or can help you find them if required.

1 Summer Activities

Whistler in summer is a great time for families, with economical choices such as biking, trail walks, and lake swims easily accessible. Children-oriented activities, programs, and packages guaranteed to keep your children busy and happy are offered by the dual mountains of **Whistler and Blackcomb** as well as by activity and tour companies. Drop by the **Whistler Activity and Information Centre,** located in the Whistler Conference Centre in Whistler Village, for information and bookings. You can also pick up a dual mountain sightseeing ticket here, which allows access to the mountains in summer. Rates are adults C$22 (US$13.75), youth and seniors C$19 (US$11.85), children 12 and under free. Summer is a lovely time of the year to visit, with comfortably warm temperatures and sunny skies.

Tips Don't Take Chances on the Mountains

Children and adults must be properly dressed for any mountaintop visit. Even if you set out from the Village on a sunny day, be aware that snow can come on suddenly in the alpine. Always come prepared, as your life could be at stake. Sneakers, a warm jacket or sweater, sun hats or caps are standard gear. Sun lotion, sunglasses, and bug spray are highly recommended.

WARM-WEATHER FUN ON THE DUAL MOUNTAINS Whistler and Blackcomb mountains (© **800/766-0449**) offer **Whistler Kids** programs for all ages. For 8- to 12-year-olds there's the skill-based **Mountain Bike Adventure Camp.** Kids can start with a beginner program or, if advanced, trails park training and descents. When it rains, the group heads indoors for activities. **Mountain Adventure Camp** for 5- to 7-year-olds offers guided hikes in the alpine and other nature-oriented options. Children learn about local trees, plants, animals, glaciers, ecology, and history. The camp includes week-long group projects. Childcare (18 months to 4 years) is available with full or half-days (mornings only) with nature walks, gondola sightseeing, outdoor play, story times, and arts and crafts, meeting at the Westin Resort & Spa Whistler. Fees not yet determined at the time of writing.

At the **Blackcomb Base Adventure Zone,** daily outdoor activities are tailor-made for thrill-seekers of all ages. Visit the All Canadian Trapeze to learn how to swing like a circus performer. At the Great Wall Climbing Centre, children can challenge several upwardly mobile routes with varying degrees of difficulty. The entire family will enjoy the Little Mountain Family Golf Centre, West Coaster Slide, or Horseback Tours.

SUMMER SKI AND SNOWBOARDING The **Dave Murray Summer Ski and Snowboard Camp** (© **604/932-5765,** www.skiandsnowboard.com) is North America's longest-running summer ski camp, with 5- and 8-day sessions from mid-June to mid-July.

Experienced 10- to 18-year-olds can spend their mornings and early afternoons skiing on the Blackcomb glacier, boarding or free-riding on the excellent terrain parks and halfpipes. Later in the day, a wide range of other outdoor activities are available. Comprehensive instruction and adult supervision earn high marks at this activity-oriented camp. Food, accommodation, and lift passes, as well as tennis, trapeze, and mountain-biking options, are included in the package. The 8-day full camp (6 days riding, 7 nights hotel) is C$1,675 (US$1,046); the 8-day local camp is C$1,395 (US$871); the 5-day full camp (3 days riding, 4 nights hotel) is C$940 (US$587); and the 5-day local camp is C$800 (US$500). **The Camp of Champions** (© **888/997-2267,** www.campofchampions.com) is the only snowboard camp on Blackcomb glacier with its own private snowboard terrain park. Having its own halfpipe, terrain park, rail park, and handle tows makes for less hiking and more riding. For 11-year-olds and up. One week at C$1,975 (US$1,325) includes accommodation. Breakfast and lunch included, but not dinners. Camp director Ken Achenbach is a member of the Snowboarding Hall of Fame.

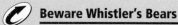 **Beware Whistler's Bears**

It's possible to see black bears almost anywhere in Whistler, on the mountains and even on the valley trails looking for berries to eat to fatten up for winter. They are most active from mid-March to November. Bears are drawn by easily available food sources, such as garbage cans, barbecues, pet food, and bird feeders. Bears that turn to garbage as a food source cannot be successfully relocated. Save a bear's life, and don't leave any food sources out in the open. In truth, bears don't enjoy encounters with humans. When out walking, warn them of your presence by talking loudly or carrying a bell or noisemaker. If you do see a bear, stay calm and back away. Never attempt to get close to a bear. And never run from one.

NATURE WALKS AND TOURS   Sightseeing, alpine hiking, and walking on Whistler and Blackcomb mountains can be enjoyed with a guide or on your own. Take the Whistler Village Gondola, and 20 minutes later you'll be on the mountaintop at 1,828m (6,000 ft.).

Whistler Mountain has seven designated hiking trails with varying degrees of difficulty. Join a tour or hire a personal guide for your group. Mountain tours are free and depart daily from the top of Whistler Mountain at 11am and 1:30pm. Free interpretive trails are also located along the west side of the Valley Trail and through the Old Mill Road in Lost Lake Park. The trails feature informative signs about Whistler's history and natural environment. The Valley Trail is made up of 25km (15.5 miles) of paved and unpaved paths that link up Whistler's five lakes. The Lost Lake Loop, 15km (9.3 miles), includes a popular beach park and peaceful forest trails.

Whistler Outdoor Experience Company offers hiking tours throughout the day (© **604/932-3389,** www.whistleroutdoor.com). If you haven't seen alpine wildflowers in full bloom, the gentle hike is highly recommended, from mid-July through August.

Finds **A Living Classroom**

The free **Whistler Interpretive Forest** is a living classroom of 7,412 acres. Elevation rises from 600m (1,968 ft.) to more than 1,600m (5,249 ft.). Its geological history shows a mix of ancient seabeds, mountain uplifting, and recent volcanoes. Six easy-to-moderate walks include the Crater Rim Trail and the Riverside Trail. Away from the bustle of the Village, quiet moments can be shared exploring the outdoors as a family.

The forest is located 3.4km (2.1 miles) south of the Whistler Visitor Info Centre across from the entrance to Function Junction. Large, paneled information signs, interpretive sites, forestry demonstrations, and other educational features are located inside the working forest area. For a free map of the interpretive forest with background material, write to the BC Ministry of Forests, Squamish Forest District, 42000 Loggers Lane, Squamish, BC V0N 3G0.

WHEELS GALORE Bring your own bicycles, skateboards, or in-line skates or rent from one of Whistler's many rental shops. The **Valley Trail** is an easygoing route for beginner activities. For more information, see chapter 6, "Summer Pursuits."

After you've whetted your appetite on the paved Valley Trail, head for the **Whistler Mountain Bike Park,** a maze of trails ranging from beginner to extreme. The bike park is located a short ride up the Whistler Village Gondola, at 1,019m (3,346 ft.). Guided mountain bike family descents will surely become the stuff of legends. Two-day fat-tire weekend camps for youths 12 to 17 are held in July and August (C$139, US$86.90), with a family fat-tire weekend in the third week of July. *Note:* Youth camps fill up early, so book well in advance. A 2-hour learn-to-ride clinic for youths is C$25 (US$15.65). Private lessons are also available. For information and registration call © **800/ 766-0449,** 604/932-3434. Visit **www.whistlerblackcomb.com** and click on **Mountain Bike Park** to check it out.

INTERNATIONAL SUMMER CAMPS   For active children who want to improve their English and enjoy real Canadian adventures such as camping and swimming, an extended stay at a summer camp is just the answer. At **Tamwood College's International Summer Camp** (© **604/938-9843,** www.tamwood.com), children can stay for 2 to 7 weeks in home-stay situations with selected Canadian families, mixing education with good times. Tamwood offers a unique English-as-a-second-language component for children with English as a second language. Junior summer programs for 8- to 17-year-olds are held in July and August, from C$2,275 (US$1,593) for 2 weeks to C$7,245 (US$5,070) for a 7-week stay. **Play Whistler** (© **604/ 932-8302**) custom-designs programs for overseas children 4 to 17 years of age, focusing on educational and cultural tours. **Whistler Parks and Recreation** (© **604/935-7529**) offers community-run day camps throughout the summer.

BOATING AND WINDSURFING   A new day, a new water experience could be the motto of Whistler Valley's five lakes and countless rivers. A host of local companies offer boating, canoeing, sailing, and kayaking, including **Whistler Sailing & Water Sports** (© **604/932-7245**), which has them all. Rafting tours for all levels, ages, and abilities with fully licensed guides are offered by **C3 Rafting** (© **604/905-2777,** www.spicysports.com) on the Green and Birkenhead rivers. You may spot eagles soaring the thermals, or enjoy a gourmet lunch. Spectacular scenery, friendly guides, and exciting whitewater await you.

Catch the wind on the west side of Alta Lake with **Whistler Kids Windsurfing** (© **604/938-8813**), whose camps and equipment are suited to individual size, strength, and ability. Three-day camps offer half-day C$135 (US$85) and full-day experiences C$225 (US$173), Mondays and Fridays, from June to the first week in September. Drop-in half-day C$60 (US$37.50); drop-in full day C$110 (US$68.75). For more information about on-the-water summer activities, see chapter 6, "Summer Pursuits."

(Value) Some Things in Life Are Free

Even the mega-resort of Whistler offers some things for free, probably because there are 9,000 local people residing in the area year-round. The valley's seven free parks and five local lakes can be enjoyed in many ways. Picnic areas, beaches, playgrounds, and washrooms are located throughout the park system. The paved Valley Trail is ideal for nature walks and biking, in-line skating and skateboarding. Many bring their own equipment up to Whistler to save rental fees. Four free public tennis courts are also available (see below).

When it's time to stroll the streets of Whistler, street entertainers and musicians are out in full force to entertain crowds free of charge from the end of June to early September. You might see fire-breathing acrobats, jugglers, clowns, or mimes. Musicians perform with fiddles, guitars, trombones, and more to get your family singing and clapping along. Some of Whistler's many festivals offer a chance for children to experience different arts and cultures free of charge. Whistler Roots Weekend, mid-June, is a pleasant mix of Celtic and bluegrass, world beat and folk, with free public performances. The First Nations Festival in August provides a stage for local aboriginal communities, including music and dance. Even Oktoberfest in mid-October features a special rootbeer hall for children.

TENNIS   Whistler Parks and Recreation (© 604/935-7529) offers tennis lessons for children, as well as four free public courts at the Myrtle Philip Community School, the Meadow Park Sports Centre, in White Gold subdivision, and behind the Fairmont Chateau Whistler parking lot. Tennis throughout the year is available at **Whistler Racquet & Golf Resort** (© 604/932-1991, www.whistlertennis.com) with three covered courts. Groupings are by age and ability, with emphasis on the basic skills and strokes of tennis. For ages 6 to 15, **Junior Tennisport Camps** are offered Monday to Friday, 9am to noon in July and August. Weekly fees are C$150 (US$93.75), a 3-day pass is C$110 (US$68.75), and a 1-day pass is C$40 (US$25).

2 Winter Activities

Given the wealth of winter activities, children are likely to try something new at Whistler. With the snow piled high, there's something magical and carefree about being in the mountains. From old-fashioned fun on a sleigh ride to individual pursuits such as snow-shoeing, winter is an appealing season. Skiing and snowboarding, as well as lessons and rentals, are available on both Blackcomb and Whistler mountains. A dual mountain pass, single-day rate for youth 18 and under is C$59.90 (US$37.50), and an adult day-pass is C$69.55 (US$43.45).

PROGRAMS FOR KIDS ON THE DUAL MOUNTAINS At **Whistler Kids** on Whistler and Blackcomb mountains (© **800/ 766-0449,** 604/932-3434, www.whistlerblackcomb.com), programs include ski and snowboard lessons with professionally trained instructors. They have a knack for getting children of all ages to tackle new challenges. **Kids Adventure Zones** feature a mystical castle, enchanted forests, secret forts, and magical animals, all designed to enchant children while helping them develop their skiing abilities. Kids-only lifts, such as **Blackcomb's Magic Carpet,** make going uphill easy. Whistler Mountain's kids-only facility **Whistler's Children's Learning Centre** provides pint-size amenities. All group programs include a full day of professional instruction and a healthy lunch. Call for a package best suited to your child and package prices. Also offered are:

Adventure Camps for kids 3 to 12 years. The 5-day C$379 (US$218) ski and snowboard camp is the most popular. Kids stay with the same group and instructor for the week, making friends and advancing skills. If you're in Whistler for only a weekend, try the Weekend Camp at C$160 (US$100), with a group of new friends and the same instructor.

Daily Children's Programs for 5 to 12 years (6 years and up for snowboard) are C$80 (US$50) and provide everything from the basics to the terrain parks to all-over exploration. All ability levels welcome. Little ones 3 to 4 years, C$84 (US$52.50), get the basics

Finds Multi-Functional Fun

The **Meadow Park Sports Centre** (📞 **604/935-7529**) is located a little way out of the Village hub, but the 5km (3.1 mile) trip north of Whistler Village on Highway 99 is worth it by car or by WAVE public transit. Conveniently, the Alpine Meadows or Emerald Estates bus stops at the front door. Built in 1992, the multi-functional sports complex has an NHL-size ice rink and heated viewing lobby. Popular public ice-skating sessions feature a "game zone" for kids. Skate rentals, helmets, and push bars are available, with qualified skate attendants offering a full-service skate shop. From April to August, in-line skating, roller hockey, and ball hockey sessions take over the rink. Highly recommended is the center's delightfully warm leisure pool with "beach access," a toddler pool, and active "river rapids," plus swim programs from toddlers to youth. In the adjacent 25m (82 ft.) six-lane pool, kids can try the rope swing, 2.4m (8 ft.) slide, and basketball net. Drop-in for adults is C$6 (US$3.75); youth 13 to 18 years C$3.50 (US$1.35), and children 4 to 12 C$3 (US$1.85). Family rate for parents and dependants under 18 is $12 (US$7.50). For all facilities, towel rental is C$2 (US$1.25).

of skiing with games that make learning fun on a specially designed children's terrain.

Infant and Toddler Care costs C$84 (US$52.50) for the tiniest member of your family, ages 3 months to 36 months, and offers fully qualified childcare specialists. A parent pager program is available, too.

Youth Programs for teens 13 to 17 years are C$80 to C$86 (US$50 to US$53.75). Beginner to expert skiers and riders who want to cut loose from Mom and Dad for the day will love the **Ride Tribe** programs. Pro instructors guide teens to the best-kept mountain secrets.

Private lessons offer individual attention and accelerated learning for ages 3 to 17 years, C$299 (US$187). These lessons offer the very best instruction for your child or your own group (up to five children of similar abilities). All abilities welcome for ski and snowboard lessons.

⟨Tips⟩ Travel Happily with Baby

No need to carry bulky equipment with you to Whistler. Baby's On The Go stocks strollers, snowsuits, toys, cribs, and all things baby (© **604/894-0092,** www.babysonthego.com). The Nanny Network (© **604/938-2823**) provides babysitters as well as equipment. Little one restless at bedtime? The **Warm Buddy Sleep Pet** at C$29.95 (US$18.70) is locally made from soft fabric stuffed with natural grain and lavender, ready to lull a lucky child to sleep. Heat it in a microwave, then tuck into bed as a warm, cuddly pal.

Kids After Hours is for those from 18 months to 12 years, 7 days a week from 4pm to 6pm at the Whistler Kids Club at the Westin Resort & Spa Whistler. Indoor games, crafts, stories, and movies are part of the fun, at C$20 (US$12.50) per child. Another option for the same age range is **Kids Night Out,** 7 days a week, evenings from 6pm to 9pm. A special children's dinner is served and indoor/outdoor games, crafts, storytelling, and movies complete the evening at C$40 (US$25) per child.

SLEIGH RIDES   Gentle giant Percheron horses with jingle bells on their show harnesses pull you through a sparkling winter wonderland, stopping to view the colorful lights of Whistler Village. **Blackcomb Sleighrides** (© **604/932-7631,** www.blackcombsleighrides. com) include a singing cowboy and hot chocolate by a roaring fire. Adults C$45 (US$28), youth 13 to 18 C$35 (US$21.80), children 3 to 12 C$25 (US$15.60), under 3 are free. Departs from Base 2 on Blackcomb Mountain 5pm, 6pm, 7pm, and 8pm. Whistler Outdoor Experience (© **604/932-3389,** www.whistleroutdoor.com) also offers fun sleigh rides for the whole family; adults C$40 (US$25), 12 and under C$20 (US$12.50), under 2 years ride free. Warm up with hot beverages and warm blankets along the Valley Trail on the shores of Green Lake. Forty-five-minute rides start at noon daily and continue until 8pm. Located at the 45-acre Edgewater Outdoor Centre, 3km (1.8 miles) north of Whistler Village, a quick trip by WAVE public transit bus or taxi.

SNOWBOARDING   For teens, Whistler Mountain's Nintendo GAMECUBE Halfpipe is an ideal place to begin exploring the dual mountains' snowboard facilities. Access the pipe by the Whistler Village Gondola, or from Creekside Gondola followed by the Red

Express chair. The park is smaller, and groomed with the regular pipe Dragon. The halfpipe on Blackcomb Mountain is much bigger and is groomed nightly with the Super Pipe Dragon.

The Nintendo GAMECUBE Terrain Park on Blackcomb is where all the action takes place. The park features an intermediate park, a snowcross track, and the Highest Level Terrain Park for experts only. The park is accessible by Wizard Express in the Upper Village, then the Solar Coaster. The terrain park is serviced by the Catskinner Triple Chair, which passes directly over the top of the Highest Level park. Park users can easily get in as many runs as they can handle while watching the experts in action. The blue park offers smaller jumps and rail slides. The snowcross track features banks, rollers, and jumps. The Highest Level park is rated double black and features much larger and more challenging rail slides. Highest Level is exclusively for advanced/expert users. Riders/skiers must sign a waiver to obtain a C$15 (US$9.35) park pass and helmets are mandatory. A parent must sign the Highest Level park waiver if the rider/skier is under 19. For more information call © **800/766-0449,** 604/932-3434, www.whistlerblackcomb.com.

SNOWMOBILING Just-for-kids snowmobile family tours are run separately from learn-to-ride tours, and have private guides to conduct each tour with **Cougar Mountain at Whistler** (© **604/ 932-4086,** cougarmountainatwhistler.com). Small children ride in safe, comfortable sleighs, while Mom and Dad ride their own snowmobile. At the cabin, children can learn to ride on the Ski Doo "Mini Z." Tours vary from 2 to 3 hours, double or single snowmobiles, C$89 (US$55.65) to C$159 (US$100), with 50% off doubling rates for children 12 and under.

SNOWSHOEING AND SNOWCAT TOURS If you can walk, you can snowshoe is the motto of Outdoor Adventures@Whistler (© **604/932-0647,** www.adventureswhistler.com). Snowshoeing is enjoying a comeback. It's simple to learn and new lightweight equipment makes the going easier. If you enjoy birds, you'll have them eating out of your hand in the easy-pace, 1.5-hour Nature/ Culture Tour. Children 12 and under accompanied by an adult are half-price. Children aged 6 and up are welcome. All tours include snowshoes, boots, and wool socks. A ski pass or a C$10 (US$6.25) sightseeing pass is required for all mountain tours. For a change of pace and a peek at the untrammeled backcountry, board the Wilderness Snowcat Tour offered by **Cougar Mountain at Whistler,**

7 minutes north of Whistler (© **888/297-2222,** www.cougar mountainatwhistler.com). Customize your family adventure with Canadian winter games such as tobogganing, snowshoeing, and building a snowman. Drink and snack included. The 3-hour tour is C$99 (US$62) for adults, children 12 and under C$79 (US$50).

 Whistler WinterFest

The resort really shines for kids at Christmas, launched by Whistler WinterStart (www.winterstart.com) held on the first two weekends in December. Teenagers flourish on the excitement of World Cup Snowboarding competitions, while younger children will enjoy Santa's Workshop and Post Office. WinterStart highlights include the very pretty Village of Light displays, glowlight parades, caroling, InterActivity Fun Zone, Meadow Park Sports Centre ice carnival, and a street hockey tournament.

Like many hotels during the Christmas holiday season, Delta Whistler Resort (© **604/932-7346**) places a special emphasis on children. In mid-December, the hotel's pastry chef hosts a gingerbread house workshop (children under 10 must be accompanied by an adult). On Christmas Day, join other families at Santa's Breakfast, a scrumptious affair for adults at C$29.95 (US$18.75), children 7 to 12 half-price, and children under 6 free. Check with individual hotels for their Christmas programs and displays.

Family Christmas activities begin early in December at the Myrtle Philip Community School. Preschoolers share breakfast with Santa, bake unique holiday treats, and make holiday crafts. Older children bake and decorate their very own Christmas mansion, make fancy gift wrap, and join a week-long **Christmas Break Day Camp.** At the Meadow Park Sports Centre's arena, **Holidays on Ice** is an event shared with the Whistler Skating Club. Children enjoy an old-fashioned Christmas skate with trees and lights, caroling, hot chocolate and goodies, plus a visit from Santa. Admission is one Canadian dollar (US$.62), better known as a loonie, and a donation to the Christmas food bank. Information for both © **604/935-7529.**

3 Children's Amenities

BAKERIES

Evergreens Bakery ☎ 604/932-1982
Husky Food Store & Deli ☎ 604/932-3959
Little Mountain Bakery ☎ 604/932-4220

BOOKS & GAMES

Armchair Books ☎ 604/932-5557
Great Games & Toys ☎ 604/932-2043
Whistler Public Library ☎ 604/932-5564

CANDY & ICE CREAM

Going Nuts ☎ 604/932-4676
Rocky Mountain Chocolate Factory ☎ 604/932-4100
Rogers' Chocolates ☎ 604/905-2462

FAMILY DINING & FAST FOOD

For more information about family dining, see chapter 4, "Where to Dine."

MOVIES

Rainbow Theatre ☎ 604/932-2422

PHARMACIES

Nesters Market & Pharmacy ☎ 604/905-0429
Pharmasave ☎ 604/932-2303, 932-4251

PHOTO FINISHING

Slalom (1 HR) Photo ☎ 604/938-9090
28 Minute Photo ☎ 604/905-0461
Whistler 1 Hour Foto Source ☎ 604/932-6612, 932-6676

VIDEO & VIDEO EQUIPMENT RENTALS

Whistler Video Tracks (videos and equipment rentals) ☎ 604/932-3540
Whistler's Other Video Store ☎ 604/932-3980

10

Side Trips

The drive from Vancouver to Whistler is only 120km (75 miles), so why rush it? Highway 99 is known as the Sea to Sky Highway, and the scenery should be savored. Along the way, typically West Coast stops include **Horseshoe Bay** for ferry watching and fish and chips. **Furry Creek Golf & Country Club** (© **604/896-2224** clubhouse, 604/896-2216 reservations and pro shop) is open for 18-hole golf as well as breakfast, lunch, and dinner, and **Britannia Beach** offers a peek at what was once a thriving copper mining town. In **Squamish,** stop and watch the rock climbers on the Stawamus Chief granite monolith, then shop for antiques. You can also golf and dine at the more affordable 18-hole **Squamish Valley Golf & Country Club** (© **888/349-3688,** 604/898-9601). Next is **Brackendale,** famous for its eagles and the area's many outdoor activities. Past Whistler, the laidback village of **Pemberton** offers the rockin' Pemberton Hotel and the best fishing around. **Mount Currie** is the gateway to the Highway 99–Duffey Lake Road route to Lillooet, as well as camping and lakes.

1 Horseshoe Bay

Thirty minutes from Vancouver, the small community of Horseshoe Bay in North Vancouver is reached by crossing either Lions Gate Bridge or the Iron Workers Memorial Bridge (also referred to as the Second Narrows Bridge), then cruising along the North Shore's Upper Levels Highway, a scenic stretch of Highway 1 West/Highway 99. At the well-marked Whistler exit, if you stay on the right, you're on the Sea to Sky portion of Highway 99. Turning left here will take you into Horseshoe Bay.

Horseshoe Bay is home to a BC Ferries terminal, with vessels en route to Vancouver Island, the Sunshine Coast, and smaller Bowen Island (good for a day trip). You'll also find restaurants and ice cream shops, gift stores, motel, public washroom, bank machine, pay telephones, and postal outlet. **The Spirit-Gallery** is open daily at

6408 Bay (© **604/921-8972**), with an impressive showing of First Nations collectible masks, prints, and jewelry. **Sewell's Marina** (6695 Nelson Ave., © **604/921-3474**) is the place to go for boat rentals, fishing, and Howe Sound tours. If you're hungry, try the famous takeout fish and chips available year-round at **Trolls Restaurant** (6408 Bay, © **604/921-7755**) for C$6.95 to C$8.95 (US$4.35 to US$5.60), or sit-down for C$8.95 to C$10.95 (US$5.60 to US$6.85) 7 days a week, 6am to 8pm. From a window seat in this family-owned restaurant founded in 1948, you can watch the ferries come and go.

Tips **Gas Up**

The next gas station is in Squamish, 44km (27 miles) north, so gas up before you leave Horseshoe Bay if need be.

---

2 Britannia Beach

Copper, not gold, was king at Britannia Beach, formerly knwn as Britannia Mines, 33km (20.5 miles) past Horseshoe Bay. During the 1920s, this now-tattered scattering of historic houses, souvenir shops, and cafes was a world center for copper, producing enough to circle the globe in half-inch copper wire 12 times. During the summer months (May to September), you can visit the **BC Museum of Mining** (© **604/688-8735**), a national historic site with 90-minute guided tours into the old mine from 10am to 4:30pm daily. Look for the giant truck parked outside. Admission is C$10 (US$6.25) for adults and C$8 (US$5) for students/seniors; children under 5 are free.

Just before the mining museum, the **Britannia House Restaurant & Tea Room** (© **604/896-2335**) has freshly baked scones, an all-day breakfast, homemade soups, and burgers. Next door is the **Ninety-Niner Restaurant** (© **604/896-2497**). The view from the two restaurants includes Howe Sound, the Coast Mountains, and the Murchison Glacier. If one isn't open, the other one usually is. A little past this, on the left-hand waterfront side, is **The Old Customs House Art Gallery** (© **604/896-2322**) with good-quality, locally made art and gifts. On the right, you'll see a turn marked by a sign "Native Arts, General Store, and Pepsi." **Native Crafts** (© **604/896-0001**) is the large and curious souvenir store housed in the old community center, with inexpensive native wall carvings and enough polished rock samples to please any rock hound. In the row of booths outside, you can buy earrings, rings, brooches, and multi-beaded necklaces from C$3 to $670 (US$1.85 to US$419) at **Amber, Silver & More,** fish and chips at **Mountain Man Fish & Chips,** or specialty takeout coffee at **Sherry's Cappucino.** The latter are not always open, subject to the season and the whim of the proprietors.

Finds **A Bathroom Break for Fido**

It's a long way from Vancouver to Whistler, and a bathroom break at Britannia Beach for yourself and your pet (if Fido is traveling with you) may be in order. At the "Native Arts, General Store and Pepsi" exit, the last on the right before leaving Britannia Beach, park in the free lot (watch for the potholes) and walk between the General Store and Lawrence's Crafts. Turn right and enter the back of Lawrence's Crafts by way of the porch and you'll find washrooms open year-round. As for Fido, cross the small pedestrian bridge over Britannia Creek and feel free to stroll with your pet along the pathway. Please remember to pick up after your pet.

---

3 Squamish

Squamish was built on logging, and events like the annual 3-day **Squamish Days Logger Sports** celebration (at the Loggers Sports Ground off Highway 99) on the first weekend in August still honor this heritage. But logging is giving way to other economic pursuits. Squamish, almost halfway to Whistler, is a bedroom community for both Vancouver and Whistler, with all the amenities that go with it, including restaurants, coffee shops, hotels, large grocery stores, souvenir shops, bookstore, gas stations, and the like.

SQUAMISH, CANADA'S RECREATION CAPITAL

As you cruise on up to Whistler, it's easy to miss Squamish's enormous recreation potential. It well deserves its self-proclaimed title of Canada's Recreation Capital. Drop by or write **The Squamish & Howe Sound Visitor Information Centre,** 37950 Cleveland Ave., Squamish, BC V0N 3G0 (© **604/892-9244,** www.squamishchamber ofcommerce.bc.ca) for a free activity and accommodations guide, including many of the local bed and breakfast spots. The visitor

Side Trips on the Sea to Sky Highway

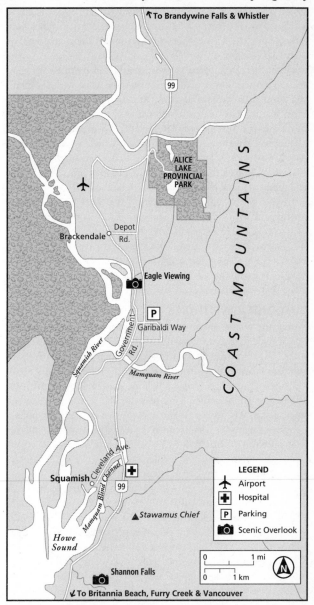

To Brandywine Falls & Whistler

99

ALICE LAKE PROVINCIAL PARK

Brackendale

Depot Rd.

Eagle Viewing

P

Garibaldi Way

Squamish River

Government Rd.

Mamquam River

COAST MOUNTAINS

Cleveland Ave.

Mamquam Blind Channel

Squamish

99

Stawamus Chief

Howe Sound

Shannon Falls

To Britannia Beach, Furry Creek & Vancouver

LEGEND

✈ Airport
✚ Hospital
P Parking
📷 Scenic Overlook

0 — 1 mi
0 — 1 km

N

center is located in the town's old railway station, with plenty of brochures to take away. Open daily June through September from 9am to 5pm; and October through May on Saturdays and Sundays from 10am to 2pm.

Visitor center volunteers will give you the run-down on the highlights of the area. Just south of Squamish is the 335m-high (1,099 ft.) **Shannon Falls Provincial Park** (no camping). The falls are a refreshing 5-minute walk through tall cedars from the free parking lot on the right off Highway 99. Includes toilets and a picnic area. Also just off Highway 99 is the **Stawamus Chief,** a sleeping granite giant 670m (2,198 ft.) high, making it the largest monolith of its type in Canada. Stop in the free parking lot and look up. Those minuscule specks are rock climbers, and they'll be there on any good day.

Another of Squamish's attractions is the **West Coast Railway Heritage Park** (39645 Government Rd., © **604/898-9336,** www.wcra.org). Here you'll find Western Canada's largest collection of heritage railway equipment, with over 60 vintage railway cars and locomotives on display year-round. Open 10am to 5pm, it costs C$6 (US$3.75) for adults, C$5 (US$3.10) for seniors and students, and kids 5 years and under free.

OUTDOOR ADVENTURES

During the winter, many outdoor activities are connected to the annual eagle festival (see below). To view eagles from a new vantage point, you can take a slowly paced rafting trip with **Sunwolf Outdoor Centre's Eagle Float Tours** (© **877/806-8046,** 604/898-1537, www.sunwolf.net) on the Cheakamus and Squamish rivers. The basic eagle float from December through February, including lunch, is C$79 (US$49.35). Sunwolf provides river rafting, hiking, and other excursions May through September. The year-round **Sea to Sky Stables** (© **604/898-3934,** www.seatoskystables.com) offers spectacular eagle viewing trail rides in Paradise Valley, 5 minutes north of Squamish, for C$69 (US$43.10). The eagles are so accustomed to the horses that you can get within a few feet of hundreds of them. Summer trail rides are C$35 to C$55 (US$21.90 to US$34.35). The three-generation-run company also has chuckwagons that sleep 12. Call for rates. **Sea to Sky Eco-Tours** (© **866/ 808-2233,** 604/898-1241, www.seatoskyadventures.com) operates all-terrain-vehicle tours of the area's backcountry from April to November. Four-hour tours are C$135 (US$84.35) for the driver, C$75 (US$48.85) for the passenger. All equipment is supplied.

The **Squamish River Estuary** is shared by hikers, bicyclists, windsurfers, kayakers, and industry. The main trail is off the end of Vancouver Street, which can be reached by driving down Cleveland Avenue. An estuary map is available from the Squamish Estuary Conservation Society, P.O. Box 1274, Squamish BC V0N 3G0. A small donation is appreciated when asking for the map. Squamish is known as a world-class windsurfing destination (see "Let It Blow" below).

Mountain biking, or simply recreational biking, is a main activity in the area. There are 63 biking trails, rated from easy to extreme. Write for a copy of The Squamish CP Guide and Business Directory (191-1524 56th St., Tsawwassen, BC V4L 2A8, **☎ 800/867-5141,** www.mapbook.com), with trail information and map.

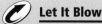 **Let It Blow**

Winds can blow in Squamish with real force, averaging 40 knots an hour on the water, with gusts as high as 70. No wonder the name *Squamish* means "Mother of the Wind" in the Coast Salish language. The powerful north winds rise before noon and blow steadily until dusk, a fact not missed by windsurfers from around the world. Windsurfing in Squamish is the best in Canada and among the top 10 venues in North America.

Access the Squamish Dyke by way of Buckley Avenue and the fisherman's entrance. Visitors must angle-park on the right side of the dyke. A daily sailing fee of C$10 (US$6.20) is charged, with a season pass of C$75 (US$45). Spectators and nonsailing family members are welcome at no charge. For wind and event information, write the non-profit **Squamish Windsurfing Society** (P.O. Box 1028, Vancouver, BC V6C 2P2), which operates the sailing park and rescue service.

DINING IN SQUAMISH

Squamish is expanding its dining possibilities and makes an excellent halfway stop en route to Whistler. Kurt Ebert is Squamish's King of Desserts at **Quinn's Restaurant & Patisserie** (38105 2nd Ave., **☎ 604/892-5560**). Or perhaps it should be desserts are king here.

Quinn's does do breakfast until 11am, and lunches with delicious main dishes such as a hot spinach and mushroom salad for C$8.80 (US$5.50), but it's the dozen other-worldly desserts in the big glass display case that will amaze you. Mile-high Black Forest cake, fresh apple torte, and chocolate cake made with pure chocolate imported from Europe are among the specialties in the C$3.95 (US$2.45) range. Open Tuesday to Saturday, 8am to 5pm. **The Howe Sound Inn & Brewing Company** (37801 Cleveland, ✆ 604/892-2603) offers good West Coast cuisine, with main courses for C$12 to C$17 (US$7.50 to US$10.60), open daily. Try steamed mussels with shallots and garlic in pale-ale cream broth, grilled lime-cured salmon steak with seasonal vegetables and Asian-style noodles, medallions of peppered venison with wild mushroom/herb glaze, or pizza topped with lime-cured chicken, Monterey Jack cheese, chilies, and tomatoes. The inn's more casual **Brewpub** also serves tasty pub grub. **Sunrise Japanese Restaurant** (40022 Government Rd., Brackendale, ✆ 604/898-2533) is open Tuesday to Sunday with a large Japanese menu. Main courses are C$6 to C$12 (US$3.75 to US$7.50). **Ian's Village Bistro** (40359 Tantalus Way, Garibaldi Highlands, ✆ 604/898-9533) features chef Ian MacDonald's amazing linguine with tiger prawns for C$14.95 (US$9.35), traditional spaghetti bolognese for C$9.95 (US$6.20), and fresh chicken breast stuffed wih apple and sage dressing for C$15.95 (US$9.95). Open for lunch from Monday to Friday; dinner from Monday to Saturday starting at 5pm. Closed Sunday. For a quick snack on your way to Whistler, drive into Squamish and try the **Sunflower Bakery Café** (38086 Cleveland, ✆ 604/892-2231), with excellent coffee and desserts baked on-site, including mountainous apple and bumbleberry pies. Their sandwiches and paninis are made with their own sourdough, multi-grain, and French loaves. Ask to have a fresh sandwich made for you.

SHOPPING IN SQUAMISH

In keeping with the growth of Squamish, there are some interesting stores along Cleveland Avenue, the main drag. Many Whistlerites shop here now for furniture, lighting fixtures, and antiques. Browse for yourself at Cobblestone Antiques (38128 Cleveland, ✆ 604/815-4471), Hidden Treasures (38036 Cleveland, ✆ 604/892-8447), The Country Store Canadiana (38041 Cleveland, ✆ 604/892-5957), Outpost Gallery (38055 Cleveland, ✆ 604/892-1080), Nothing Finer (38016 Cleveland, ✆ 604/892-6366), and Billie's Bouquet (38082 Cleveland, ✆ 604/892-9232). The Emerald Gift

Box (38028 Cleveland, ✆ **604/815-4438**) stocks reasonably priced, quality local pottery platters and salad bowls hand-painted with fanciful images as well as vintage denim jeans with Indian silk appliqués. **Mostly Books** (38012 Cleveland, ✆ **604/892-3912**) is a small but good bookstore with a well-chosen selection of the works of local writers as well as bestsellers.

WHERE TO STAY IN SQUAMISH

For an overnight stay, try the **Howe Sound Inn & Brewing Company** (37801 Cleveland, ✆ **800/919-2537,** 604/892-2603, www.howesound.com). Here you'll find 20 excellent units starting at C$95 (US$60) from October to April; and to C$105 (US$66) from May to September for a double, with free parking. The beautiful new wood-and-stone lodge has queen-size beds, cozy comforters, a reading lounge, and sauna. There's also the 52-unit **Best Western Sea to Sky Hotel** (40330 Tantalus Way, ✆ **800/531-1530,** 604/898-4874), with double occupancy rooms at C$89 (US$55.60) per night. A suite that sleeps six is C$109 (US$68) per night double occupancy, plus C$10 (US$6.25) extra per person over 17 years of age. Suites have two TVs, small bar, fridge, and microwave. At the well-established, quiet motel **August Jack Motor Inn** (37947 Cleveland, ✆ **604/892-3504**), rates start at C$65 (US$41) for single occupancy, doubles at C$69 (US$43) for one bed, C$75 (US$47) for two beds. The six-unit **Squamish Hostel** (38490 Buckley Ave., ✆ **604/892-9240**) offers a year-round fun, social atmosphere for backpackers, climbers, mountain bikers, international travelers, and others traveling on a budget, with both dorms at C$15 (US$9.30) and private rooms that can sleep two at C$30 (US$18.75) for a total of 18 occupants. Check for its new location right off Highway 99 in Squamish in the late summer of 2002. The new hostel will have six private rooms with showers and bathrooms as well as dorm rooms, and will house 50 guests. Reservations for a larger group are advised.

The **Coneybeare Lodge B&B** (40549 Ayr Dr., ✆ **866/815-9299,** 604/898-9299, www.coneybearelodge.com) has spectacular mountain and forest views from a choice of two fully appointed and luxurious private guest rooms, each with its own balcony. The upper room is C$125 (US$78), and the double, lower room is C$115 (US$72). There's also a family suite for up to four people with its own entrance and self-service breakfast for C$90 (US$56.25). This is a very well-done B&B, with swimming pool, poolside sauna, large soaker tub, fine linen and goose-down duvets, and a delicious gourmet breakfast.

Hosts Jim and Claire Harvey personally guide visitors on some of the area's best mountain bike terrain and hiking trails.

For something completely different, with no television or telephone but plenty of wilderness ambiance, stay in a riverside cabin at the **Sunwolf Outdoor Centre** (70002 Squamish Valley, Brackendale *€* **877/806-8046,** 604/898-1537, www.sunwolf.net). Located on over 5 acres at the confluence of the Cheakamus and Cheekye rivers, the 10 beautifully renovated units (some with kitchenettes) give you a front-row seat for bird watching, eagle viewing, or just plain vegging out. All cabins feature cathedral ceilings, gas fireplaces, fir floors, and handcrafted pine furniture, which includes both a double and single bed. You will definitely feel the flow. The basic cabin is C$90 (US$56.25), and the cabin with kitchenette is C$100 (US$62.50). Sunwolf also arranges eagle watching, fishing, hiking, rock climbing, kayaking, mountain biking, and horseback riding tours.

All Squamish area accommodations are subject to a 15% tax.

Fun Fact **First Nations Residents**

Before Europeans came to the Squamish Valley, the area was inhabited by the Squohomish tribes. They lived in the North Vancouver area and came to the Squamish Valley to hunt and fish. The first contact with Europeans occurred in 1792, when Captain George Vancouver came to the area to trade with First Nations people near what is now Brackendale. In the early 1900s, 16 Squamish reserves amalgamated under the Squamish Indian Band. Cheakamus (River) means "salmon weir place," and Cheekye (River) is said to come from the name for Mount Garibaldi, meaning "dirty place," perhaps due to the appearance of old snow on the mountain. The meaning of Mamquam (River) is uncertain, but may be inspired by the sound of a smooth-flowing river. On the left off Highway 99 before Squamish, look for the totem pole outside Totem Hall, the band's community center. On the right of Highway 99 is the Squamish Nation's gift shop, south of the bridge over the Stawamus River and close to the Stawamus Chief. For more information call *€* **604/892-5166.** Mount Currie north of Pemberton is also home to some 1,000 First Nations people.

4 Brackendale

Tenkm (6.2 miles) north of Squamish is one of the earliest settlements in the valley. Brackendale was named after John Bracken, the owner of the Bracken Arms Hotel, built in 1908 and burned down in 1917. Today, Brackendale is known for its **Annual Bald Eagle Count and Festival,** drawing thousands of spectators between November and February. Festival founder Thor Froslev, curator of The Brackendale Art Gallery, Theatre and Teahouse at 41950 Government Rd., corner of Depot Road (© **604/898-3333,** www.brackendaleart gallery.com), leads walking tours to eagle-viewing sites during this time. An official count takes place on the second Sunday in January, starting at the art gallery. Turn off Highway 99 at Brackendale, 10km (6.25 miles) past Squamish. Signs point the way to Government Road. An official count takes place on the second Sunday in January, starting at the art gallery. On Saturdays, Sundays, and holidays throughout the year explore the art gallery and teahouse, supping on four different kinds of soups served with bread, starting at C$5.50 (US$3.45), or croissants with spreads for C$4.25 (US$2.65), noon to 8pm. **The Brackendale Café** (41703 Government Rd., © **604/898-9211**) is a mom-and-pop cafe, with chef William's hearty turkey pies at C$5.50 (US$3.45) available for takeout. Open Mondays to Fridays from 8am to 5pm, weekends from 7am to 5pm.

Moments **The Majesty and Power of Eagles**

No sight quite matches that of hundreds of majestic eagles soaring overhead, feasting on salmon or perching atop cottonwood trees. If you visit Brackendale from November to mid-February, you'll share the awe felt by visitors and photographers from around the world. Nearly 2,000 bald eagles were counted in January 2002 by rafters, hikers, canoeists, and kayakers observing the eagles gathered to feed on chum and salmon in the Squamish River. First Nations people, including the local Skomish First Nation, regard eagles as symbols of power and spirituality. Seeing an eagle is a sign of good fortune.

For an accessible view of the eagles, head for the **Eagle Watch Interpretive Centre** located on a walkable dyke along the Squamish River. Exit off Highway 99 at the Garibaldi Highlands, turning left onto Garibaldi Way. At Government Road, turn right to the Easter

Seals Camp. Free parking is available. From the end of mid-November to mid-February, volunteer wardens are on hand Saturdays and Sundays (9:30am to 3:30pm) to answer questions and share binoculars and spotting scopes. *Note:* Cloudy days and rainy days make for the best eagle viewing. The birds prefer to roost rather than fly around. Dress warmly, as the southerly winds along the river are chilly.

For more on ways to see the eagles, see "Outdoor Adventures" below.

5 North of Whistler

PEMBERTON

For a simpler taste of British Columbia, head north to **Pemberton,** 25km (15.5 miles) beyond Whistler. Like Squamish, Pemberton is a fast-growing bedroom community of Whistler. Set in the broad, flat Pemberton Valley at the base of the imposing 2,590m (8,497 ft.) Mt. Currie, Pemberton was originally the ideal center for farming and ranching. Workers in these two industries now coexist with visitors who are attracted by the area's many outdoor activities, and workers commuting to Whistler jobs.

Unlike Squamish, Pemberton still has a small-town feel, with a main street that you can walk in 3 minutes. Small it may be, but Pemberton has a lot to offer. From mid-June to September, the **Pemberton Infocentre** (✆ **603/894-6175**), located across from the Petro-Canada gas station on Highway 99, is a good place to learn about the area. The **Pemberton Chamber of Commerce** (✆ **604/ 894-6175**) can also help with information, including accommodations such as bed and breakfasts. Ask about mountain biking, alpine hiking, fishing, climbing, heli-skiing, helicopter sightseeing, cross-country skiing, boating, hang-gliding, rodeos, alpine lakes, river rafting, jet boating, kayaking, hunting, wildlife viewing, hot springs, and arts and crafts. Outfitters include the well-established **Adventure Ranch** (1642 Sea to Sky Hwy. 99, ✆ **604/894-5200**) with a summer season program of rafting and horseback riding. Wild Bill's Trail Rides (✆ **604/894-5182, cell 604-938-4288**) is 18km (11 miles) north of Pemberton on Meadows Road. If you like to do it yourself, stop in at the **Spud Valley Sporting Goods** store (✆ **604-894-6630,** www.spudvalley@msn.com) at 1380 Birch St., 7 days a week for fishing, hunting, camping, and general sports needs, including rentals. The staff know the area, and can advise on the best places to fish, hike, or bike. Area topographic maps are also for sale.

Squamish & Brackendale

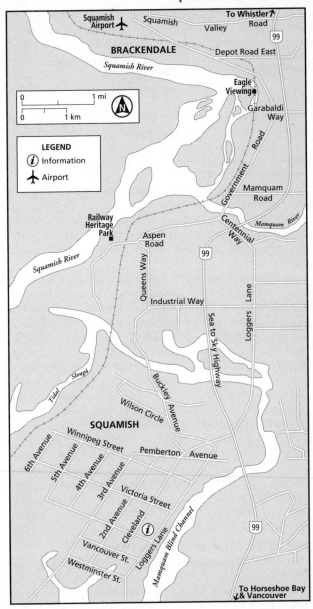

Pemberton has two 18-hole golf courses, the world-class **Big Sky Golf & Country Club** (1690 Airport Rd., ✆ **604/894-6106**) and the more affordable **Pemberton Valley Golf & Country Club** (1730 Pemberton Airport Rd., ✆ **604/894-6197**).

To enter Pemberton, turn off Highway 99 on Portage Road. On your left, you'll quickly spot the **Pony Espresso** (1426 Portage Rd., ✆ **604/894-5700**). If you're in the mood for a quick, cheap nosh such as soup and bagels, this tiny cafe will suit you. If you also want to rub shoulders with low-maintenance outdoorsy types and find out the best place north of Whistler to snowboard or mountain bike, this is where you'll do it. Past the Pony Espresso is a small mall with the new **Pemberton Trail Steakhouse** (1392 Portage Rd., ✆ **604/894-3340**), a nicely appointed, casual place to have lunch or dinner. In the same small mall is **Coyote Arts & Crafts** (4-1384 Portage Rd., ✆ **604/894-6900**), with felted wool scarves hand-stitched with native motifs such as the raven and hand-crafted items from around the world. There's also a good selection of local native silver jewelry and bead work.

Drive on a few blocks into Pemberton proper. Park for free on Main Street near the railway station, and stroll about town, stopping at **The Pemberton Hotel Cafe** (7423 Frontier St., ✆ **604/894-6313**) for a more than adequate breakfast from Monday to Saturday to 11am, Sunday to 1pm, for C$6 to C$12 (US$3.75 to US$7.50); lunch at C$7.95 to C$9.95 (US$5 to US$6.29); or dinner, including specials, which may be a pasta dish, Mexican- or Asian-inspired fare, a prime rib dinner, roast lamb, or fire-grilled steaks, from C$12.95 to C$15.95 (US$8.10 to US$9.95). In addition to a small smoking lounge with keno, bingo, and karaoke, there's a large pub seating 150 patrons where excellent live bands play on weekends. The friendly proprietors of the **Centennial Café** (7439 Frontier St., ✆ **604/894-6433**) serve up Chinese, Japanese, and Canadian food. For groceries to take back to Whistler, or with you on a camping trip even farther north, the **Pemberton Valley Supermarket** (7438 Prospect, ✆ **604/894-3663**) has organic free-range chicken, a good selection of deli meats, fresh-baked French breads, and a soup and sandwich snack for only C$5 (US$3.10).

WHERE TO STAY IN PEMBERTON

Close to Whistler but quieter, Pemberton is also a popular summer destination for its many outdoor activities or for just taking it easy. Established in 1914, the historic **Pemberton Hotel** (7423 Frontier St.,

(✆ **604/894-6313**) has rooms on the second floor. A non-smoking double is C$79.95 (US$49.95), renovated double C$89.95 (US$56.20), smoking double C$69.95 (US$43.70). Outdoor parking is free. The town also has several lovely bed and breakfast residences. The 464 sq. m (5,000 sq. ft.) **Loghouse B&B Inn** (1357 Elmwood, ✆ **800/894-6002,** 604/894-6000, www.loghouseinn.com) has seven guest bedrooms. All bedrooms in this impressive log home have private or en suite bathrooms, TVs, bathrobes, and toiletries provided. Guests enjoy a full cooked breakfast featuring local farm produce. There's also an outdoor hot tub on the deck and a large guest lounge with wood-burning fireplace. It's located on the hill behind the village, a short walk to amenities. Low season is October to November, May to June, C$85 to C$115 (US$53 to US$72); high season is C$105 to C$185 (US$65.60 to US$116). No pets. Children on request. Hosts are Donna and Saad Hasan.

A 15% tax is added to all accommodations.

Fun Fact **As Pure as the Driven Seed Potato**

Virus-free Pemberton seed potatoes make their way to growers around the world. Twenty-eight tonnes of seed potatos are grown on every one of the 200 hectares (494 acres) in production, on average 40,320 plants per hectare. Being hemmed in by mountain ranges has protected Pemberton seed potatoes from virus-carrying aphids. So when you're anywhere in Canada, in the potato-growing states in the United States, or as far afield as South Korea, China, Sri Lanka, Peru, Saudi Arabia, Scotland, or South Africa, you may be munching on produce grown from starters from "the seed potato capital of North America."

MOUNT CURRIE

Six km (3.7 miles) north of Pemberton is the small village of Mount Currie, population 1,400, and home to the 1,000-strong Interior Salish Lilwat group of the Stl'atl'imx (pronounced stat-lee-am) Nation band. The old part of the reserve intermingles with the non-native part of the village and includes some houses that are a century old. A new housing development, Xit'olacw, is 4km (2.4 miles) off the highway and you are unlikely to visit it except by invitation. Towering Mt. Currie is a sacred mountain for the local people.

Lil'wat members in Mount Currie organize two rodeos over the May and September long weekends. For more information call © **604/ 894-6115.**

Mount Currie remains small, but like the rest of the Sea to Sky Highway it's growing gradually. You'll find restaurants and gift stores selling original First Nations arts and crafts, and two gas stations. You'll also find **The Wicked Wheel Pizza Co.** (2021 Portage Rd., © **604/894-6622**), with its delicious pizzas famous even with locals in Whistler.

If you're driving through Mount Currie to Lillooet along Highway 99 you'll pass through the village first, making a sharp right turn at the old wooden church. Another choice is to continue straight through Mount Currie on Pemberton Portage Road to the Birkenhead Lake Provincial Park (see "Provincial Parks & Private Campgrounds" below).

Tips Gas Up Before It's Too Late

Both Pemberton and Mount Currie have gas stations, an important convenience to note. Make sure to gas up if you're driving on to Lillooet 100km (62 miles) down the road. Once you're on the 85km (53 mile) Duffey Lake Road (as the highway between Mount Currie and Lillooet is known) you leave civilization behind as you cautiously climb the Duffey Lake (Cayoosh) Pass through the Coast Mountains at over 1,300m (4,265 ft.). The descent into Lillooet at 230m (754 ft.) above sea level is not for the faint of heart or those without good brakes. This is as wild as it gets: no gas station, no accommodations, no emergency telephone, no cafes until you reach the town of Lillooet. You can camp en route though, as well as use the rough-and-ready outhouses along the way.

---

6 Provincial Parks & Private Campgrounds

You don't have to search hard for parks and campgrounds along the Sea to Sky Highway. Provincial parks (and a host of rustic recreation sites) make the most of the Coast Mountain range's lakes, waterfalls, and mountain vistas. Fifty-five provincial parks lie in the Garibaldi/ Sunshine Coast District. Fees range from limited services at C$12 (US$7.50) to full service at C$18.50 (US$11.55), maximum four people in a group over the age of 16. Children under 16 years are free. Firewood is free. For more information on provincial parks, contact **BC Parks Visitor Services,** P.O. Box 220, Brackendale, BC V0N 1H0 (© **604/898-3678,** www.elp.gov.bc.ca). To reserve a campsite, call **Discover Camping** after March 1 at © **800/689-9025,** 604/689-9025. To reserve online after March 1, go to www.discover camping.ca. A fee of C$6.40 (US$4) is charged per night for your reservation for a maximum of three nights. Reservations are recommended. Domestic pets are not permitted in all parks, so inquire if kitty is coming along. You can also camp at several privately run campgrounds along Highway 99.

PROVINCIAL PARKS

Alice Lake Provincial Park   Thirteen km (8 miles) north of Squamish, 108 campsites. A very popular camping area, with four warm-water lakes. Free hot showers, flush toilets, and a sani-station. Hiking trails, picnic areas, sandy beaches, swimming areas, and fishing spots are on the grounds. It's C$19 (US$13) per night for a walk-in or drive-in site.

Birkenhead Lake Provincial Park   Thirty-two km (20 miles) past Mount Currie on Pemberton Portage Road, 18km (11 miles) off road to park facilities. A serene park with 91 campsites, wood supplied, toilets, litter barrels, boat launch, drinking water, day parking, a sandy beach, and family swimming. There's excellent fishing in the 6km (3.7 mile) lake stocked with rainbow trout, Dolly Varden, and kokanee. You may see moose, deer, black bears, martens, bobcats, and river otters. You can also fish on the Birkenhead River for chinook and Coho salmon, Dolly Varden, steelhead, and rainbow trout.

Brandywine Falls Provincial Park   Thirty-seven km (23 miles) north of Squamish, with 15 campsites. Natural features include the 66m (216 ft.) namesake falls, Daisy Lake, and mountain views of Garibaldi Provincial Park. Hiking and sightseeing. Firewood is available. Open April to November.

Garibaldi Provincial Park   There are five well-marked access areas off Highway 99: Diamond Head, Black Tusk, Cheakamus Lake, Singing Pass, and Wedgemont. The park, boasting a total of 196 wilderness/walk-in sites, was created in 1920 to protect the 2,678m (8,786 ft.) Garibaldi Mountain. The park's 480,000 acres are located in the Pacific Ring of Fire, an extensive arc of volcanic activity. No need to worry—nothing has erupted locally for 2,400 years. The park includes temperate rain forests as well as alpine glaciers. You can hike, camp, mountaineer in the backcountry, ski, snowboard, and cross-country ski. Look for frozen rivers of glacial ice, debris from volcanic activity, alpine meadows, wildlife, and birds.

Meager Creek Hotsprings *(Overrated* Gives new meaning to "off the beaten track." It takes real fortitude to get to the hot springs, 70km (43 miles) down a narrow, rocky, and dusty road when it's at its best. The rest of the time it's impassable. But diehards do go there, for the geothermal waters (52°C to 100°C) and for the rugged isolation of the backcountry. From Pemberton, follow the paved Pemberton Meadows Road through farmlands. At the 28km (17 mile) point, the pavement ends. Turn right at the Coast Mountain Outdoor School turnoff, crossing over the Lillooet River Bridge. Continue on the gravel road that flows along the Lillooet River. At the Mile 24 marker, turn left and continue a few km beyond, watching for a sign at the parking lot. The roads are best from June to September. In winter, take chains and ski in part of the way. Avoid the area altogether in spring and fall, when heavy rains obliterate the road. Landslides are possible in the area, and killed four geologists in 1975. For more information, call or write Squamish Forest Service (42000 Loggers Lane, Squamish, BC V0N 3G0, *©* **604/898-2100**) for a free map of the Meager Creek Hotsprings recreation site and trail.

Murrin Provincial Park Three km (1.8 miles) north of Britannia Beach, south of Squamish. Day use only, no camping. Includes two lakes. Fishing, swimming, hiking, picnics. Rock climbers make the most of the steep cliffs visible on the side of Highway 99.

Nairn Falls Provincial Park Twenty-eight km (17 miles) north of Whistler, with 88 campsites. The 60m (196 ft.) Nairn Falls tumble into the Green River. Pit toilets, drinking water, and firewood available. Hiking, fishing for rainbow and Dolly Varden trout, and Green River rafting are popular. Swim in One-Mile Lake, 2km (1.2 miles) north on Highway 99. Open from April to October.

Porteau Cove Provincial Park Twenty-five km (15.5 miles) north of Horseshoe Bay with 44 campsites. Scuba divers can explore artificial reefs made from hulls of sunken ships. Firewood available.

PRIVATE CAMPGROUNDS

Dryden Creek Resorts   1796 Depot, Brackendale, just off Highway 99 (_©_ **604/898-9726**). Year-round facility with motel rooms as well. Twenty-four RV sites for C$24 (US$15) with full hookups. Twenty tent and RV sites with no hookups for C$11.25 (US$7.05). Pets allowed. Wood is C$2.50 (US$1.55) a bucket. Showers, washrooms.

Klahanie Campground & RV Park   Highway 99 across from Shannon Falls south of Squamish (_©_ **800/767-0830,** 604/892-3435). Year-round with 100 sites. RV sites with full hookups, a sani-station, washrooms, and laundry facilities. Tenting and RV sites with no hookup are C$19.50 (US$12.50), including tax, RVs with electricity and water are C$22 (US$13.75), RVs with electricity, water, and sewer are C$24 (US$15). Based on double occupancy. C$3 (US$1.85) extra per person 12 years and older. Pets are C$5 (US$3.10) per night, per pet. Wood is C$6.50 (US$4.00) per box. Extra parking is C$3 (US$1.85) per day. The on-site Roadhouse Diner is open to the public for breakfast, lunch, and dinner.

Riverside RV Resort and Campground   In Whistler, 8018 Mons Rd., 1.8 km (1.2 miles) north of Whistler Village next to Highway 99 at Spruce Grove Park (_©_ **877-905-5533,** 604/905-5533, www.whistlercamping.com). Open year-round. Sixty-seven serviced and winterized RV sites are C$35 (US$21.90), 31 tent sites are C$20 (US$12.50), 14 cozy log cabins are C$125 to C$150 (US$78.10 to US$93.75). Cabins include queen bedroom, two-person loft, pull-out couch, kitchen, and bathroom. Kids under 16 in a family unit are free. Leashed pets welcome for nightly guests (not in cabins). Convenience store, cafe, laundromat, and recreation room.

Index

See also Accommodations and Restaurant indexes, below.

NOTES

NOTES

NOTES

NOTES

NOTES

NOTES

FROMMER'S® MEMORABLE WALKS

Chicago	New York	San Francisco
London	Paris	

FROMMER'S® GREAT OUTDOOR GUIDES

Arizona & New Mexico	Northern California	Vermont & New Hampshire
New England	Southern New England	

SUZY GERSHMAN'S BORN TO SHOP GUIDES

Born to Shop: France	Born to Shop: Italy	Born to Shop: New York
Born to Shop: Hong Kong, Shanghai & Beijing	Born to Shop: London	Born to Shop: Paris

FROMMER'S® IRREVERENT GUIDES

Amsterdam	Los Angeles	San Francisco
Boston	Manhattan	Seattle & Portland
Chicago	New Orleans	Vancouver
Las Vegas	Paris	Walt Disney World
London	Rome	Washington, D.C.

FROMMER'S® BEST-LOVED DRIVING TOURS

Britain	Germany	Northern Italy
California	Ireland	Scotland
Florida	Italy	Spain
France	New England	Tuscany & Umbria

HANGING OUT™ GUIDES

Hanging Out in England	Hanging Out in France	Hanging Out in Italy
Hanging Out in Europe	Hanging Out in Ireland	Hanging Out in Spain

THE UNOFFICIAL GUIDES®

Bed & Breakfasts and Country Inns in:	Southwest & South Central Plains	Mid-Atlantic with Kids
California	U.S.A.	Mini Las Vegas
Great Lakes States	Beyond Disney	Mini-Mickey
Mid-Atlantic	Branson, Missouri	New England and New York Kids
New England	California with Kids	New Orleans
Northwest	Chicago	New York City
Rockies	Cruises	Paris
Southeast	Disneyland	San Francisco
Southwest	Florida with Kids	Skiing in the West
Best RV & Tent Campgrounds in:	Golf Vacations in the Eastern U.S.	Southeast with Kids
California & the West	Great Smoky & Blue Ridge Region	Walt Disney World
Florida & the Southeast	Inside Disney	Walt Disney World for Grow
Great Lakes States	Hawaii	Walt Disney World with Kids
Mid-Atlantic	Las Vegas	Washington, D.C.
Northeast	London	World's Best Diving Vacation
Northwest & Central Plains		

SPECIAL-INTEREST TITLES

Frommer's Adventure Guide to Australia & New Zealand
Frommer's Adventure Guide to Central America
Frommer's Adventure Guide to India & Pakistan
Frommer's Adventure Guide to South America
Frommer's Adventure Guide to Southeast Asia
Frommer's Adventure Guide to Southern Africa
Frommer's Britain's Best Bed & Breakfasts and Country Inns
Frommer's Caribbean Hideaways
Frommer's Exploring America by RV
Frommer's Fly Safe, Fly Smart
Frommer's France's Best Bed & Breakfasts and Country Inns
Frommer's Gay & Lesbian Europe

Frommer's Italy's Best Bed & Breakfasts and Country Inns
Frommer's New York City with Kids
Frommer's Ottawa with Kids
Frommer's Road Atlas Britain
Frommer's Road Atlas Europe
Frommer's Road Atlas France
Frommer's Toronto with Kids
Frommer's Vancouver with Kids
Frommer's Washington, D.C., with Kids
Israel Past & Present
The New York Times' Guide to Unforgettable Weekends
Places Rated Almanac
Retirement Places Rated